# Scholastic WRITING Workshop

## Crafting STORIES

SUE ELLIS,
ANNE HUGHES
& LYNDA KEITH

# Scholastic WRITING Workshop

**Published by Scholastic Ltd,**
**Villiers House,**
**Clarendon Avenue,**
**Leamington Spa,**
**Warwickshire CV32 5PR.**
Text © 1996 Sue Ellis, Anne Hughes and Lynda Keith
© 1996 Scholastic Ltd

234567890   78901234

**Project Consultants**
Sue Ellis and Gill Friel

**Authors**
Sue Ellis, Anne Hughes and Lynda Keith

**Editor**
Clare Gallaher

**Assistant Editor**
Kate Pearce

**Series Designer**
Joy White

**Designer**
Sue Stockbridge

**Illustrations**
Sue Woollatt

**Cover illustration**
Patrice Aggs
(From *Mr Pam Pam and the Hullabazoo* by Trish Cooke, Walker Books Ltd)

Designed using Aldus Pagemaker
Printed in Great Britain by Bell & Bain Ltd, Glasgow

British Library Cataloguing-in-Publication Data
A catalogue record for this book is available from the British Library.

ISBN 0-590-53470-X

# Contents

**5 Chapter One**
## INTRODUCTION

**11 Chapter Two**
## ASSESSMENT

**23 Chapter Three**
## CHARACTERISATION

**67 Chapter Four**
## PLACE AND SETTING

**99 Chapter Five**
## STORY STUCTURE

**139 Chapter Six**
## THE WRITING PROCESS

**161 Chapter Seven**
## USING THE STORY BOOKS

# ACKNOWLEDGEMENTS

The publishers gratefully acknowledge permission to reproduce the following copyright material:

David Higham Associates for 'Sounds in the Evening' from *Silver Sand and Snow* by Eleanor Farjeon © Eleanor Farjeon (published by Oxford University Press); Tony Mitton for 'Rain Rhymes' from *Scholastic Collections: Early Poems and Rhymes*, compiled by Jill Bennett © 1993, Tony Mitton (1993, Scholastic Ltd); Penguin Books Ltd for extracts from *Patch The Pirate Cat* by A. Martyr and P. Lawford © A. Martyr and P. Lawford (Hamish Hamilton); *Lazy Jack* by Tony Ross © Tony Ross (Puffin) and *Can Piggles Do It?* by Frank Rogers © Frank Rogers (Viking Children's Books); *Starting School* by Janet and Allan Ahlberg © Janet and Allan Ahlberg (1988, Viking Children's Books); Mathew Price Ltd for an extract from *Jumble Joan* by Rose Impey © Rose Impey (1989, Ragged Bears); Random House UK Ltd for permission to use an extract from *Katie Morag and the Tiresome Ted* by Mairi Hedderwick © 1986, Mairi Hedderwick (1986, Bodley Head); Scholastic Ltd for the use of an extract from *Dulcie Dando* by Sue Stops © 1990 Sue Stops (1990, Andre Deutsch); Walker Books for permission to use text extracts from *Mr Pam Pam and the Hullabazoo* by Trish Cooke © 1994 Trish Cooke illustrated by Patrice Aggs (1994, Walker Books Ltd); Westwood Creative Artists (Toronto, Canada) and Michael Bedard for an extract from *The Lightning Bolt* by Michael Bedard © Michael Bedard (1989, Oxford University Press, Canada). Andersen Press for the use of the cover illustration from *Paul's Present* by Philippe Dupasquier © 1992, Philippe Dupasquier (1992, Andersen Press, London SW1V 2SA); HarperCollins Publishers Ltd for the use of text and illustration from *The Brick Street Boys: Here are the Brick Street Boys* by Allan and Janet Ahlberg. Illustration © Janet Ahlberg (1992, Collins); Penguin Ltd for the use of an illustration from *Knock, Knock Who's There?* by Sally Grindley © 1985 Anthony Browne (1985, Magnet Books); Scholastic Ltd for the use of an illustration from *A Scary Story* by Peter Bailey, illustrated by Peter Bailey 1993 © Peter Bailey (1993, Andre Deutsch); from *Alex's Bed* by Mary Dickinson, illustrated by Charlotte Firmin; for permission to use illustrations © 1993 David Parkins from *Blooming Cats* by David R. Morgan illustrated by David Parkins (1993, Hippo Books); Walker Books for permission to use illustrations © 1994 Patrice Aggs from *Mr Pam Pam and the Hullabazoo* by Trish Cooke © Trish Cooke illustrated by Patrice Aggs (1994, Walker Books Ltd).

Scholastic
IMAGINATIVE WRITING
Workshop

Scholastic
WRITING
Workshop

*Chapter One*

# INTRODUCTION

# TEACHING THE CRAFT OF STORY WRITING

If our teaching is to be an art, we must remember
that it is not the number of good ideas that turns our
work into an art, but the selection, balance and
design of those ideas.
(Lucy Calkins, *The Art of Teaching Writing*)

This resource has been developed to help teachers teach imaginative writing in a way that:
• is flexible and responsive to the children's needs and interests;
• is reflective and analytical, focusing on key issues in teaching and learning;
• results in children who are confident, enthusiastic writers, who write stories because they find it a challenging and satisfying pastime.

## Teaching writing

In recent years there has been much research on how young children learn to write. This has drawn attention to the different kinds of thinking involved in writing and to the importance of the emotional dimension of writing and learning. Key issues are identified below, but the introduction to the *Story Projects* book explores some of these in more depth.

The writing process perspective developed by the work of Donald Graves and Lucy Calkins has emphasised the importance of purpose, context and audience in writing, and has drawn teachers' attention to the process as well as the product.

Researchers working from the emergent literacy perspective have detailed the wealth of experience and knowledge of print that young children bring to school, and have shown how infant teachers can capitalise on this to develop confident and knowledgeable writers by making clear what the child needs to know.

There has also been a lot of recent work on the nature and importance of stories. The 'real books' debate did much to identify the key elements of a story – that stories contain characters, settings and problems to be resolved. Developmental psychologists have emphasised how children learn to 'story' experience and the part this narrative plays in the construction of understanding.

To teach imaginative writing, teachers need to consider the child as both a story-maker and a story writer. Relatively little is known about how young children's knowledge of imaginative writing develops – how they develop and synthesise the quite specific skills and knowledge required for writing stories or how teachers can best help them to acquire the craft knowledge this requires.

Teachers have been given much advice on story topics, on purpose and audience in writing and on creating contexts that are exciting and meaningful. However, they have been given little specific help with the teaching content of story writing, or on how to ensure an appropriate balance and coverage.

## Subject knowledge, context and young children

The publication of the National Curricula for England and Wales and for Northern Ireland and the 5–14 Guidelines for Scotland has drawn attention to the role and organisation of subject-focused knowledge in the primary school curriculum. The trend has been towards a subject focused, non-integrated curriculum. This has led specialists in Early Years education to decry the 'death of infancy' (Blenkin and Kelly, 1994) and the declining emphasis on meaningful learning contexts and general processes. Teachers of young children need to harness enthusiasm for learning and help children to learn how to learn. They need to work with the children's interests and establish a broad base of experience and understanding by encouraging connections between home and school, work and play. A focus that is solely on subject–content does not easily lend itself to this.

# SCHOLASTIC WRITING WORKSHOPS

The *Scholastic Writing Workshops* have been produced in the belief that:
• *Content knowledge is important.* Teachers need to provide a broad and balanced range of opportunities for children to experience, so that they develop understanding and skill in the different aspects of story writing. This includes both the writing processes and the craft techniques that writers use.
• *Context is important.* Learning contexts need to be exciting and meaningful and build on the children's existing knowledge of storytelling

and writing. Teachers need to know how and when home experiences, play experiences and collaborative work can support aspects of story writing. They need to use these, along with observation and discussion, to develop and deepen specific knowledge, understanding and skills.

• *Process is important.* Teachers need to create a classroom ethos that values children's work and fosters the writing process so that children become enthusiastic and confident writers who take a pride in their work.

*Scholastic Writing Workshops* provide resources for sustained story projects and for ensuring that children experience a broad and balanced range of shorter writing activities through which they can explore specific techniques and skills.

The resources provide teachers with:
• the content knowledge and analytical framework;
• the contexts to generate stories and writing;
• guidance on how to assess and respond appropriately to young writers.

### Why use a workshop approach?

The term 'workshop' reflects beliefs about the nature of writing and the nature of learning to write – that writing is both a practical and an intellectual activity. A basic organising principle of the workshop approach is that everyone will be involved in both individual and collaborative efforts. The writing workshop approach involves teachers and children in setting goals, in modelling ways of working, in giving advice, support and encouragement and, most importantly, in listening to the ideas of others and providing a sounding-board that helps them clarify what they want to say and what they know.

### What is needed for the workshop approach?

The approach is flexible and does not require a particular form of classroom layout or organisation. It lends itself to composite classes and team teaching situations.

The workshop materials allow teachers to be responsive to children's needs and interests in selecting the most appropriate contexts and balance. This helps to create the supportive enthusiastic environment in which children learn best.

Teachers may need to consider how to use the available display space for writing and think about the degree to which the children could be involved in deciding where and how their work should be presented. If children are to take responsibility for presenting their work, they will need to be taught systematically the basic principles and skills of design and layout.

### Individual work and group work

The *Scholastic Writing Workshop* activities involve children working individually, in pairs and in small groups. Children undoubtedly need space and silence to work on their own stories and to develop their own style. However, work with others can both support and deepen children's learning. Collaborative work can:
• deepen motivation and involvement;
• help children to organise their thoughts;
• help children to understand what the reader needs to know;
• provide a sounding-board for ideas;
• help children to organise their thoughts;
• deepen understanding by making thoughts explicit;
• deepen understanding by expressing knowledge in their own terms;
• promote independence, originality and diversity within the class;
• illustrate strategies for generating and developing ideas;
• promote confidence, self-awareness and sensitivity.

## COMPONENTS OF THIS WORKSHOP

### *Crafting Stories*

A teachers' resource book providing:
– ideas for short activities that prompt children to focus on different aspects of stories and story-writing techniques. Teachers can plan a teaching programme that targets different techniques for characterisation, place and setting, structure and the writing process;
– ideas and lesson plans for using picture books by professional authors to encourage children to discuss and reflect on the writer's craft.
– photocopiable activity sheets;
– photocopiable anthology pages;
– suggestions, advice and photocopiable pages for assessment and record-keeping.

## The writing activities

The activities have been designed to enable teachers to target children in Key Stage 1 of the National Curricula for England and Wales and Northern Ireland, and Levels A–B of the English Language 5–14 Guidelines for Scotland.

The following information is given by symbols at the beginning of each activity:

*Level of difficulty* is indicated by a star rating. Activities with one star are the easiest in terms of content level and the amount of support given. Three-star activities are the most difficult and are aimed at older or more experienced children. Where the content or type of activity is new, one-star activities provide starting points for all children.

*Class organisation* shows whether the activity involves children working individually, in pairs, in groups or as a class.

*Time required* gives an idea of how long each session may take. Obviously, this can only be a rough guide and much depends on individual teachers and classes.

The activities are then laid out clearly under the following headings:

*Teaching content* explains the main teaching point of each activity.

*What you need* details at a glance the resources required for the session, including any photocopiable pages and photocopiable anthology pages that can be used in the activity.

*What to do* explains each activity and how to raise particular issues for discussion.

*Further development* gives ideas for taking the activity further, or for applying it to different contexts. Picture books may be listed, which illustrate or develop the ideas in the activity. Teachers may draw children's attention to these in the class library.

## Photocopiable anthology pages

These are photocopiable pages of poetry, fiction and illustrations linked to specific activities. They extend children's experience of quality literature and can be used to promote discussion, and develop or improve children's reading–writing skills.

## *Story Projects*

A teachers' resource book providing:
– ideas and lesson plans for 12 extended writing projects;
– photocopiable activity sheets;
– ideas for presentation and publishing of children's work;
– suggestions, advice and photocopiable pages for assessment and record-keeping.

## The children's books

The eight high-quality children's books support work in the chapter entitled 'Using the story books' in *Crafting Stories*. They have been selected to provide examples of fine writing that are accessible and enjoyable for the whole class. The stories contain situations and themes which are relevant to children of all ages.

It is important for young story-makers to think about the characters, settings and structure of the stories they read because it begins to establish a framework for talking about books and writing. However, such discussion should never be at the expense of enjoying the story for its own sake. Teachers will find that many children can be encouraged to make connections between their own stories and those in books. If done sensitively, this can be a powerful tool for learning.

The books included in this workshop are:
*Knock Knock Who's There?* by Sally Grindley and Anthony Browne
*Blooming Cats* by David Morgan
*A Scary Story* by Peter Bailey
*Get Lost, Laura!* by Jennifer Northway
*The Garden* by Dyan Sheldon and Gary Blythe
*The House Cat* by Helen Cooper
*Ruby* by Maggie Glen
*Mr Pam Pam and the Hullabazoo* by Trish Cooke

## The audio cassette

The 45-minute audio cassette contains readings of the eight children's books. These readings by professional actors enhance the quality of the children's experiences of the books by supporting the use of the stories in a variety of classroom contexts. Children can choose to listen to the taped stories with or without the text; they can listen alone or with friends, or within specified work groups. Teachers may therefore use the tapes to generate general enthusiasm and interest in the books, or as a basis for a more focused examination of the text.

# USING THE SCHOLASTIC WRITING WORKSHOPS

## Classroom management and planning

The *Scholastic Writing Workshops* are a resource, not a scheme. Each teacher and class is unique, and teachers should use the workshop materials in the way that is best for them and the children they teach.

Only the teacher can decide when children will benefit from focusing on specific story aspects or techniques using activities from this volume. The sustained contexts from the *Story Projects* book support and target clusters of craft aspects but also allow children time to 'live' with a story, to discuss it with friends and become emotionally committed to writing it well.

Some teachers may plan the work of the class around a succession of the story projects, interspersing them with individual one-off activities from *Crafting Stories* to ensure a balanced coverage. Other teachers may plan a number of individual activities centred around a particular aspect of a story and run a story project as a mini-break with the class.

## Where do I start?

Where to start depends on the interests, experience, attitudes and writing needs of the class. The *Story Projects* volume contains collaborative writing tasks and play activities which encourage children to work together and become involved and enthusiastic about their stories. The projects can be good starting points:
- if the class or teacher is new;
- if the children are not particularly keen on writing;
- if the children have not done much extended writing.

The sustained nature of the story projects provides opportunities for the teacher to observe the children and to learn from what they do and say. Teachers may immediately recognise activities that will address specific needs or appeal to particular interests.

If the class are enthusiastic storytellers and writers, the teacher may target particular aspects of a story, using activities from *Crafting Stories*.

This allows exploration of specific techniques which match the children's immediate interests and needs as writers;
- the time available;
- the format and content of forward plans in other curricular areas.

## Planning across year groups

The graded activities on characterisation, setting and structure help teachers to plan appropriate work for the different groups in a class and to ensure progression from one year-group to the next. School staff will need to discuss the balance between writing projects and the shorter activities focused on the craft aspects. However, whole-school policies must ensure that individual teachers retain sufficient autonomy and flexibility to plan an appropriate and balanced scheme of work that meets:
- the children's needs as storytellers and writers;
- the children's interests;
- the time available;
- the issues being addressed in other curriculum areas.

## Bibliography

Kress, G. (1982) *Learning to Write*, Routledge
Graves, D. (1989) *Experiment with Fiction*, Heinemann
Blenkin and Kelly (1994) 'The Death of Infancy', *Education 3–13*, 10/94
Calkins, Lucy McKormick (1986) *The Art of Teaching Writing*, Heinemann

## KEY TO SYMBOLS

level of difficulty of the activity

(35) approximate duration of the activity in minutes (a blank clock indicates an untimed activity)

photocopiable page for classroom use

† each child in the group working individually

†† children working in pairs

†††† a small group collaborating

W whole class or larger group working together

## TEACHING CONTENT

| | Imaginary descriptions | Real descriptions | Detail in descriptions | Structuring descriptions | Emotional reaction and mood | Speech and dialogue | Covers and titles | Beginnings and endings | Viewpoints | Generating and planning strategies | Audience | Authorship |
|---|---|---|---|---|---|---|---|---|---|---|---|---|
| **CHARACTERISATION** | 1,2, 6,7, 9, 17, 18, 19, 21 | 3,4, 8, 13, 14, 20, 24 | 3,4, 5,8, 12, 14, 15, 18, 19 | 3, 16, 22 | 5,9, 13, 14, 15, 23 | 10, 11, 12 | | | | | | |
| **PLACE AND SETTING** | 1,8, 9, 10, 11, 12, 14, 18 | 3,4, 5,6, 20 | 1,2, 3,4, 7,8, 9,11, 14, 18, 21, 22 | 4,5, 6 | 7,13, 15, 17, 21, 22 | | | | | 2,9, 11 | | |
| **STORY STRUCTURE** | | | | 1,2, 4 | 12, 18 | | 7,8, 9, 10, 11, 12 | 13, 14, 15 | 16, 17, 18 | 2,3, 4,5, 6 | | |
| **THE WRITING PROCESS** | | | | | | | | | | T1, T2, T3,1, 2 | T6, 2,9, 10, 11, 12, 13 | T5, T6,3, 4,5,6, 7,8 |

*Note:* These numbers refer to activity numbers.
T = Teachers' activities

# Scholastic WRITING Workshop

## *Chapter Two*

# ASSESSMENT

# ASSESSMENT

Assessment is to be based on what pupils say and do as well as what they write and on observations of how they go about their tasks and activities. It's purpose is to promote learning and encourage learners.
(Dignen, Morrison and Watt, 1994, 'Learning in the Early Years Curriculum', *Early Education: The Quality Debate,* Scottish Academic Press)

This section should be read in conjunction with the section on assessment in the *Story Projects* resource book.

## Assessment of writing

Assessment in the *Scholastic Writing Workshops* is used to:
• help teachers select appropriate learning activities;
• help children celebrate their stories and progress;
• help children to become aware of what they know so that they can draw on it in future.

To teach effectively and accurately target the children's needs, teachers must explore and assess the thinking that underpins each child's work. It is not enough simply to focus on a piece of writing – a teacher needs to know:
• why the child told the story in this way;
• which parts were difficult or easy;
• how the child feels about the story;
• which parts the child thinks are successful or weak, and why.

For example, assessment of a child's understanding of characterisation should be informed by what the child says when discussing stories she has read and by what she says and does in play as well as through her writing. Teachers need to combine information from all these sources to judge where and how to 'pitch' the teaching.

## Progression in writing

Progression in all aspects of writing is complex. All children will have evolved personal strategies for telling stories, be they through play, conversation or writing. Teachers should look for evidence of progression in the stories children write, but also in those they play and tell.

Progression may be seen in terms of the child's ability to:
• use a broader range of strategies;
• tell a wider range of types of stories;
• be more aware of what they, and other writers do, and how.

## General assessment and record-keeping photocopiable pages

Five types of generic assessment and record-keeping systems are provided in this book. They are intended to complement those in the *Story Projects* resource book. Teachers should use those which they find most helpful.

### Class/group notes (pages 14-16)

The class/group notes are intended as an informal record for the teacher's personal use. They provide a format for teachers to remind themselves of children who stood out during each lesson and why. Children may stand out for a number of reasons:
• because they found something hard or easy;
• because they said or did something which showed insight;
• because they produced a surprising story;
• because they showed particular enthusiasm or reluctance, sudden understanding or lack of it during the activity.

The format reflects the organisation of the workshop materials into the three aspects of characterisation, setting and structure, and the strategies associated with each. Teachers should photocopy relevant sheet(s) and, as the class or group complete activities, simply jot down under the relevant section the date, activity number and any notes about the class or individuals.

As activities are added, the class/group notes provide a useful basis for future planning because they:
• provide a running record of what has been covered;
• show the overall balance of learning activities at a glance;

• provide a rough record of how the class in general, and some children in particular, coped with the work.

The class/group notes also allow teachers to spot children who feature very regularly or, just as importantly, do not feature at all. If particular names keep cropping up, teachers must consider whether the work is pitched at an appropriate level for these children. Similarly, if some names never feature, teachers will want to be sure that this is not because these children are being overlooked.

The activities in the writing process chapter are not covered by class/group notes because the writing contexts in the *Story Projects* resource book provide a more appropriate frame work in which to observe and assess the process.

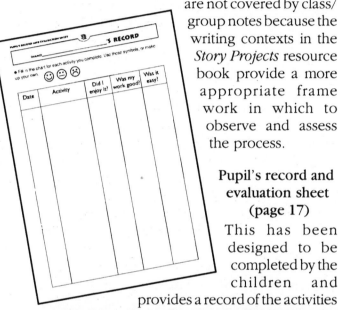

### Pupil's record and evaluation sheet (page 17)

This has been designed to be completed by the children and provides a record of the activities covered by each child, along with an indication of the child's response in terms of interest/enjoyment, level of difficulty and achievement. It can highlight individual learning patterns or attitudes and has been designed to be attached to the back of each child's writing jotter or folder, so that it can be completed while each activity is fresh in the child's mind. The list of work can be used for children to reflect on their writing over a period of time.

### Writing review form (page 18)

This form has been designed to encourage children to look reflectively at their writing. It provides both a forum and a format for the child and teacher to

assess the child's writing development over a period of time, highlighting strengths and successful learning experiences.

The form provides a format for children to review all their work – published stories from the *Story Projects* and the shorter pieces written in response to activities in *Crafting Stories* – and to reflect on their progress to date.

This may be particularly useful before a parents' evening or home report. The form can be filled in by the teacher in conversation with the child.

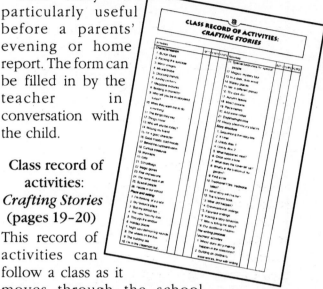

### Class record of activities: *Crafting Stories* (pages 19–20)

This record of activities can follow a class as it moves through the school, providing a record of what has been covered in each year. It can help teachers to find a starting point with a new class and facilitate progression from one year-group to another.

### Teachers' audits (pages 21–22)

Writing down what is known about the writers in a class and the range of writing experiences which they have had in the recent past can help teachers to find a starting point for the class. It allows gaps in the teacher's knowledge of the children, or in the children's experience, to be identified and filled. Photocopiable page 21 provides headings to help teachers audit their knowledge of individuals in the class. Photocopiable page 22 provides an audit sheet for the recent story-writing activities undertaken by the class. This enables the teacher to assess the breadth of experiences the children have had.

# CHARACTERISATION

## Strategies

Characterisation through appearance:

Characterisation through action:

Characterisation through speech:

Character study:

# PLACE AND SETTING

## Strategies

Vocabulary, detail and structure of description:

Creating places:

Emotive descriptions:

# STORY STRUCTURE

## Strategies

Sequencing the plot:

Beginnings and endings:

Titles, layout and divisions:

**(NAME)**_____ **'S RECORD**

◆ Fill in the chart for each activity you complete. Use these symbols, or make up your own. ☺ ☺ ☹

| Date | Activity | Did I enjoy it? | Was my work good? | Was it easy? |
|------|----------|-----------------|-------------------|--------------|
|      |          |                 |                   |              |

**(NAME)**_____**'S WRITING REVIEW**

This is how I feel about my writing:

I am much better at

I am proud of

The next time I write I want to try to

My favourite piece of writing that I did is

because

# CLASS RECORD OF ACTIVITIES: CRAFTING STORIES

| Activities | R/P1/ | Y1/P2 | Y2/P3 | Activities | R/P1/ | Y1/P2 | Y2/P3 |
|---|---|---|---|---|---|---|---|
| **Characterisation** | | | | 11. Special bedrooms for special people | | | |
| 1. Button clues | | | | 12. Magical mystery tour | | | |
| 2. Packing the suitcase | | | | 13. In a dark, dark wood | | | |
| 3. Mirror images | | | | 14. Watery places | | | |
| 4. My wardrobe | | | | 15. Me in different places | | | |
| 5. Choosing friends | | | | 16. The dark den | | | |
| 6. Jumbly pictures | | | | 17. Autumn leaves | | | |
| 7. Magazine pictures | | | | 18. Music dreams | | | |
| 8. Building a character | | | | 19. Place-names | | | |
| 9. Who will you be in storyland today? | | | | 20. Add some detail | | | |
| 10. When they want me to do something... | | | | 21. Daytime/night-time | | | |
| 11. The things they say | | | | 22. Happy places/scary places | | | |
| 12. Things I hear | | | | **Story structure** | | | |
| 13. Who will you be today? | | | | 1. Sequencing the story-line | | | |
| 14. Missing my friend | | | | 2. If I met... | | | |
| 15. I'm a good character! | | | | 3. Untidy Alex 1 | | | |
| 16. Good moods, bad moods | | | | 4. Untidy Alex 2 | | | |
| 17. Behind the cupboard doors | | | | 5. What happened next? | | | |
| 18. Curious creatures | | | | 6. Once upon a time | | | |
| 19. Wallpaper | | | | 7. What does the cover tell us? | | | |
| 20. Gifts | | | | 8. What's at the bottom of the garden? | | | |
| 21. Schoolbags | | | | 9. Find a title | | | |
| 22. Magic gloves | | | | 10. Traditional titles, traditional tales? | | | |
| 23. First impressions | | | | 11. What story will this be? | | | |
| 24. The name says it all | | | | 12. The scariest book | | | |
| 25. Special people | | | | 13. What *did* happen? | | | |
| 26. People in our school | | | | 14. Conversational endings | | | |
| **Place and setting** | | | | 15. Fairy-tale endings | | | |
| 1. I'm thinking of a place | | | | 16. Making a story collection | | | |
| 2. My favourite place | | | | 17. Who is telling the story? | | | |
| 3. 'But my school has...' | | | | 18. Our dad/those children | | | |
| 4. The view from my door | | | | **The writing process** | | | |
| 5. Through the window | | | | *Teachers' activities:* | | | |
| 6. Holiday places | | | | 1. Where does story-making happen in the classroom? | | | |
| 7. Night sounds/morning sounds | | | | 2. Building on children's experiences; links with writing | | | |
| 8. The wheels on the bus | | | | | | | |
| 9. The building site | | | | | | | |
| 10. I'm in the classroom but... | | | | | | | |

| Activities | R/P1/ | Y1/P2 | Y2/P3 | Activities | R/P1/ | Y1/P2 | Y2/P3 |
|---|---|---|---|---|---|---|---|
| 3. Identifying what children know – review of observations | | | | *A Scary Story* | | | |
| 4. Teaching techniques – self-audit | | | | 1. My own scary story | | | |
| 5. How could I set up and develop a writing area? | | | | 2. Eyes everywhere! | | | |
| 6. What's available in the classroom to motivate children to write? | | | | 3. If I *met* the scary ghost... | | | |
| | | | | 4. If I *was* the scary ghost... | | | |
| | | | | 5. In the torchlight | | | |
| 7. Where does children's writing go? | | | | 6. Safe at last? | | | |
| *Children's activities:* | | | | *Get Lost, Laura!* | | | |
| 1. Night-time stories | | | | 1. Our story about Laura | | | |
| 2. Stories, stories everywhere (but which could I use best?) | | | | 2. When I was little | | | |
| | | | | 3. Lost! Stories of the search | | | |
| 3. Favourite writing places | | | | 4. I don't like it when others tell me... | | | |
| 4. My first story | | | | | | | |
| 5. What I like best about writing is... | | | | *The Garden* | | | |
| 6. Feelings about writing | | | | 1. She had never seen anything quite like it before... | | | |
| 7. How has your writing improved? | | | | 2. From the centre to the edge | | | |
| | | | | 3. Night sky/morning sky | | | |
| 8. Storytellers I have known | | | | 4. A dream | | | |
| 9. Important people, important opinions | | | | 5. The original American people | | | |
| | | | | *The House Cat* | | | |
| 10. The writer's wall | | | | 1. The way home | | | |
| 11. Critical friends | | | | 2. Snapshots of school | | | |
| 12. Poster adverts | | | | 3. Could I find my way home? | | | |
| 13. Where do my stories go? | | | | 4. The reflection in your eyes | | | |
| *Using the story books* | | | | *Ruby* | | | |
| *Knock Knock Who's There?* | | | | 1. Ruby is an interesting bear | | | |
| 1. Who's behind the door? | | | | 2. What kind of bear is Ruby? | | | |
| 2. If you come in here | | | | 3. My special toy | | | |
| 3. Funny feet and fitting shoes | | | | 4. Escape | | | |
| 4. Where I live | | | | *Mr Pam Pam and the Hullabazoo* | | | |
| *Blooming Cats* | | | | 1. Food for a king; food for Mr Pam Pam | | | |
| 1. Words, pictures and layout | | | | 2. Pam Pam knocking on your door! | | | |
| 2. Another title, another story | | | | | | | |
| 3. Dedications | | | | 3. The storytellers | | | |
| 4. First and last | | | | 4. Pam Pam looking for new clothes! | | | |
| 5. Cat talk | | | | 5. Moving like a Hullabazoo | | | |

# TEACHERS' AUDIT SHEET 1

| Children's names | Stories enjoyed: in play; reading and writing | Attitudes and feelings about writing | Use of characterisation; place; structure |
|---|---|---|---|
| | | | |

# TEACHERS' AUDIT SHEET 2

| List of recent story-writing activities | Was this activity about: | | | |
|---|---|---|---|---|
| | Characterisation? | Place/setting? | Structure? | Writing process? |
| | | | | |

Scholastic WRITING Workshop

*Chapter Three*

# CHARACTERISATION

# INTRODUCTION

## Why is characterisation important?

Young children are fascinated by characters. When they read stories, it is the characters that make them care about what happens and prompt them to think about, discuss and re-enact the story. This fascination with characters can motivate and help children to write – when they have a clear idea of *who* the story is about, they are better able to decide what the characters do and what happens, and they become emotionally involved in writing.

The characters in stories provide a glimpse of another person's experience and view of the world. In noticing how and why story characters are similar and different, children learn about others and also about themselves. Story characters can give children security about who they are.

## What do children know about characters and characterisation and how do they show this?

*Children know about real-life characters.* They meet lots of different people who look, act and speak in various ways. Toddlers know that people react differently and demand different responses, and they exploit this in fairly sophisticated ways; two-year-olds are adroit in selecting where, when and with whom to have their tantrum – they know for example, that it is more effective in public, at the supermarket checkout, than to have it alone at home!

*Children know about the characters on television and videos.* Television, videos and advertisements all expand children's knowledge and experience of characters. These characters are often larger than life – the characteristics are magnified to ensure that young children distinguish them. Children quickly learn to recognise and interpret these and the stereotypical characters that result. This has a ripple effect: they begin to notice these features when they are not so exaggerated and use the broad elements to classify characters they meet in other stories and in real life.

If children experience a range of different types of television and video programmes, the media can be a powerful learning device: through it, children can encounter a range of different types of character and it can draw their attention to the broad elements of how to convey character.

*Children know about characters in books.* Stories exist about every kind of character. These characters may be real people in real situations like the *Alfie and Annie Rose* stories by Shirley Hughes; real characters in fantasy situations like *On The Way Home* by J. Murphy; or fantasy characters engaged in magical or fantastic adventures. In stories, the character is created from a powerful combination of the pictures, the words and the reader's imagination.

Exposure to different versions of a well-loved story can teach children to see characters in different ways. They learn to develop their own preferred images and to be aware that different writers and illustrators imagine and portray the characters differently. This lays the foundation for understanding that each writer has a unique story to tell and must present an explicit picture to the reader.

## How do children show what they know?

• Through play:

Children demonstrate a knowledge of characterisation in their play. Whether they play with other children, puppets, small figures, farm animals or dinosaurs, they bring the characters to life by giving them voices, speech, actions and roles, creating or imagining the necessary artefacts. They know that to be a princess they need a crown and fancy clothes and must walk and talk in a regal fashion. They also experiment with differences between characters; perhaps one princess adopts an air of disdain for lesser mortals and another is good, sweet and kind.

• Through drawings:

When children draw they often make sure that the physical detail concurs with their view of what the character is like. When they talk about their drawings they highlight the features that are important – 'This dinosaur has a *really* long neck because it eats people.'

• Through talk:

When children talk about or retell stories, they use the right voices, actions and speech patterns. They have opinions on what the characters are like and will say, for example, 'She's the oldest because she's wearing white trainers' or 'He's really bad because he has bushy eyebrows.'

## Unlocking children's knowledge for writing

The challenge for the children and for the teacher is to recognise that the detailed information about characterisation that is generated in play is also required when writing stories. This involves four areas of potential difficulty.

*The character is unclear in the child's mind.* Some children begin writing with only a very superficial idea of their characters. They have a general impression, but have not thought about them in sufficient depth to clearly envisage how the character looks, speaks or would react to events in the story. In play, such children often work out these details as the story unfolds and are helped and prompted to do so by their peers. A few can also manage to do this for themselves as they write, but many more need time to discuss and elaborate the characters before they pick up a pencil. Providing opportunities for this can help to ensure that stories are rich, vivid and emotionally satisfying for both the reader and writer. The more children think about their characters, the more real they become. As the characters become real to the children, their emotional involvement in their stories grows.

*The child focuses on the action, not the characters.* Sometimes young children are so keen to get the exciting part of a story down, they do not think about the characters at all. They write a story that is so devoid of human interest, it reads like a report. The actions are listed in sequence and detail, but the absence of character means that, for the reader, the events are poorly explained and linked. These children need to be encouraged to focus on the characters, to draw them, talk about them and act them out at the start of the story before they begin to write.

*Children know about their characters but they don't always tell the reader.* When children are writing stories that are vivid and exciting, they forget that the reader does not share their insider's view. Some children fail to appreciate what the reader needs to know. In play or discussion, the audience is immediate and will ask questions or say when they don't understand. But the reader is not present when stories are written. Some children need support and discussion to help them reread their stories (often aloud) so that they can see what sense they make to the reader.

Other children get caught up in the immediacy of the story that they are creating. They don't take time to fill in the detail that the reader needs because they live the story as they write it and their desire to get to the end and see what happens forces the pace.

*Children don't know how to show the*

*characterisation.* In play, characterisation is often demonstrated through actions, noises or gestures – all of which cannot be immediately reproduced in a written story. Writers use a variety of techniques for portraying characterisation in their stories.

---

• Through appearance:
He was the smartest pirate in all the Seven Seas. His boots were always highly polished and his trousers were always neatly pressed...
(*Patch the Pirate Cat* by A. Martyr and P. Lawford)
• Through speech:
'Gormless beetle brain!' screeched his mother. 'You should have carried it in your arms.'
'Okay,' said Jack. 'I'll do so next time.'
(*Lazy Jack* by Tony Ross)
• Through actions:
It wasn't as if Piggles liked watching everything on TV. Some of the programmes were awful. Piggles just couldn't be bothered to switch it off.
(*Can Piggles Do It?* by Frank Rodgers)
• Through environments and lifestyles:
Every morning and every evening this little old man walks down his street, from the little silent house where he lives alone, past the small row of shops, through the park where the children have fun and into the playground of the closed-down school where once he was caretaker.
(*Blooming Cats* by David R. Morgan)

---

The teaching programme should encourage children to use and explore all these ways of portraying characters, giving children a broad and balanced experience to develop both their understanding of how to portray characterisation in writing and their skills in using such techniques.

## Teaching characterisations

In teaching characterisation, therefore, the teacher needs to:
• *plan for a variety of characters.* Children need to be encouraged to think about using a variety of different sorts of characters in their stories: characters from their lives, characters they have invented but who are realistic, and fantastical, magical characters. The ability to invent a range of characters depends to a large degree on familiarity with different types of stories. They need to be encouraged to enjoy (through playing, reading and watching) characters from a wide variety of story genres

if they are to have the confidence and knowledge to write about similar people of their own invention.

• *teach different techniques for characterisation.* Teachers also need to frame writing lessons to ensure that, over a period of time, children are shown techniques they could use for characterisation in their stories. This means the teaching programme must provide a balanced and broad range of activities that introduce and explore characterisation through appearance, actions, speech and environments/lifestyles. Children need experiences in which they both think about and write using these different aspects.

• *give children time and strategies to develop rounded characters.* If the key characters are hazy in the children's own minds they will be absent, or at best two-dimensional, in the story. Teachers need to ensure that the sequence of writing lessons focuses children on the characters at an early stage and provides opportunities for them to make the characters 'come alive'. This may involve playing, art, drama, drawing or writing to make children think and talk about what their characters are like. Because their characters are more real and they have 'lived' with them for longer, they begin to care about them and to explore different aspects of their personality. The characters begin to shape and drive the story.

• *help the children to imagine the reader.* Obviously, the children need to know that they are writing stories for others to read. They need to watch their stories being read by others and to listen to the readers' appreciation and questions, for it is this, ultimately, that will underpin their understanding of the power and pleasure of writing.

However, it is also vital that young children find writing stories a joyful and emotionally satisfying experience. Often, the pleasure of the story lies in telling it. The drive to tell the story is all powerful and many young children find it difficult, both emotionally and intellectually, to revisit and recast their work in the light of a reader's comments.

Young children do need to understand what the reader needs to know, and many of the difficulties they experience in writing are because they assume knowledge the reader does not have. However, help and advice about the reader's understanding (or lack of it) is most useful *during* the writing process, when the child is making decisions about what to say in the story. Feedback and questions are

not helpful if unwilling children are then made to cycle back and review what they have written. Cajoling reluctant children into revising their stories is a negative experience for both the teacher and the children and is unlikely to have a positive effect on the understanding, or enjoyment, of writing.

• *use a range of teaching contexts including the children's experience as readers.* Characterisation need not be taught and discussed solely in the context of the stories children personally write. Discussion of the characters in other people's stories, both those of professional writers and of other children, can often provide the necessary emotional distance for identifying good ways to make the character come alive, and for identifying what the reader needs to know and what the readers feel like when they do not understand.

Through reading the work of their peers, children learn to link reading and writing and to see how their knowledge as readers can be applied to their work as writers.

• *respond to the child, not the product.* Teaching input is useful before and during the writing session. It is much less useful when children have finished.

Where characterisation is weak in a finished story, it is not always helpful for the teacher to respond by requesting a child to add more detail about the character. Without a major rewrite, the child ends up adding physical descriptions or repeating those descriptions that are already in the story, but with more emphasis – 'It's a big giant, a really big giant.' The result is that the story gets longer, but not more interesting or vivid. The opportunity to show the character through speech and dialogue, action and environments has been missed, along with the opportunity for the character to drive the story-line.

Once it is finished, a story needs to be celebrated and enjoyed for what it is. Obviously, the teacher will analyse the characterisation, plot and setting and find out what the child thinks is most and least effective. This information should be used to inform the future content and structure of lessons, ensuring that next time the child writes he or she is supported in thinking about those aspects that are most problematic.

# CONTENTS AND ORGANISATION

This chapter has been organised into five main sections.

## Characterisation through appearance

This is often the aspect of characterisation that children and teachers focus on most readily in story writing. Young children need opportunities to explore the links between appearance and character and to build up the vocabulary and skill to describe the important physical details of real-life, imaginary and fantasy characters. They need to recognise how and when stereotyped characteristics are useful and when they are not.

## Characterisation through speech

Young children need to develop an ear for the voices and speech patterns they hear around them every day and be encouraged to use these in their writing. Through being encouraged to use direct speech in their stories, children will learn when and how dialogue can be effective and they will also build up the necessary experience that enables them both to get into dialogue and to get out of it and back to the narrative of the story.

## Characterisation through action

'Actions speak louder than words' is an old but true adage. Many young children love to put action into their stories, but often this is in terms of what happens and has a minimal relationship to the characters.

Young children find it difficult to realise that they have a choice about how their characters respond and that writers use this to illuminate the characters. However, if this understanding is to develop, the seeds need to be sown. Young children need to be encouraged to notice that people behave differently and to think about how their specific characters would respond to the different situations they invent. In this way, children can be encouraged to learn about their characters *as* they write and this can lead to an understanding of character change as the story unfolds.

## Characterisation through friends and environments

The friends and environments against which characters are portrayed can underline aspects of a character, either by contrast which throws them into sharp relief, or by mirroring them which deepens and strengthens the impression given to the reader. Young children need to see the connection between characterisation and environments and to appreciate the different ways in which writers use this to tell their stories.

## Integrated characterisation activities

These activities offer young children opportunities to focus on or use more than one of the above aspects, proving an important opportunity for them to think about whole characters and make their own decisions about how they will tell the reader about them.

## Bibliography – children's books

*On The Way Home*, J. Murphy (1982) Macmillan
*Patch the Pirate Cat*, A. Martyr and P. Lawford (1992) Picture Corgi
*Lazy Jack*, Tony Ross (1987) Puffin
*Can Piggles Do It?*, Frank Rodgers (1991) Viking

| Activity | Teaching content | Star rating | Group size | Photo-copiable |
|---|---|---|---|---|
| **CHARACTERISATION THROUGH APPEARANCE** | | | | |
| 1 Button clues | Clothes can indicate type of character | ** | W↔2↔4 | |
| 2 Packing the suitcase | Characterisation through dress | * | W/4 | ✓ |
| 3 Mirror images | Clothes, actions and mannerisms contribute to characterisation | */** | 4↔2 | |
| 4 My wardrobe | People dress differently | ** | W↔1 | ✓ |
| 5 Choosing friends | People make choices based on clues from appearance and actions | **/*** | 1↔2 | ✓ |
| 6 Jumbly pictures | The reader expects certain characters to wear certain clothes | **/*** | 4↔1 | ✓ |
| 7 Magazine pictures | Thinking about a broad range of characters | *** | 1 | ✓ |
| 8 Building a character | Describing faces | *** | W↔2↔W | ✓✓✓ |
| **CHARACTERISATION THROUGH SPEECH** | | | | |
| 9 Who will you be in storyland today? | Characters react and speak differently | * | 1↔4 | ✓ |
| 10 When they want me to do something... | Speech differences in people we know | */*** | W | ✓ |
| 11 The things they say | Developing an ear for differences in speech patterns | **/*** | W↔2 | |
| 12 Things I hear | People speak differently in different situations | *** | W↔1 | A |
| **CHARACTERISATION THROUGH ACTION** | | | | |
| 13 Who will you be today? | Writers need to imagine how others speak and behave | * | 4 | |
| 14 Missing my friend | Personal qualities and characteristics are more important than appearance | */*** | 1 | |
| 15 I'm a good character | People can have different views of the same person. Seeing yourself as an individual | */*** | W↔1 | ✓ |
| 16 Good moods, bad moods | Actions indicate mood and characterisation | **/*** | W↔1 | |
| **CHARACTERISATION THROUGH FRIENDS AND ENVIRONMENTS** | | | | |
| 17 Behind the cupboard doors | Environments indicate character | **/*** | W↔1 | ✓ |
| 18 Curious creatures | Creating characters to suit setting | */** | 4↔1 | ✓ |
| 19 Wallpaper | Characters have different preferences and make different choices | */*** | 1 | ✓ |
| 20 Gifts | Characters have different preferences | */*** | 1 | ✓ |
| 21 Schoolbags | Character accessories indicate general and specific aspects of character | **/*** | 1 | ✓ |
| **INTEGRATED CHARACTERISATION ACTIVITIES** | | | | |
| 22 Magic gloves | Inventing imaginary characters and powers | */*** | 4↔1 | ✓ |
| 23 First impressions | First impressions are not always correct | **/*** | 1 | |
| 24 The name says it all | Names are important for characterisation | ** | W↔2 | ✓ |
| 25 Special people | Characterisation through action, speech and appearance | *** | W↔1 | ✓ |
| 26 People in our school | Describing characters in real life | **/*** | 2 | |

A = photocopiable anthology page
W = whole group

## 1
## BUTTON CLUES

### Teaching content

Small details on clothes can indicate the lifestyle or occupation of the owner. This can help to form a description of the person.

### What you need

A variety of buttons (for example, shiny or glittery buttons, pearl buttons, crystal buttons, wooden and leather buttons, novelty buttons in the shape of animals, sweets, houses and so on, any large unusual buttons), a large tin button box, several smaller boxes or baskets, writing and drawing materials.

### What to do

Gather the class together and show them the large button box. Open the lid and show them the pile of buttons inside. Take out a handful of buttons and let them fall slowly back into the tin. Tell the children that over the years you have found lots of unusual buttons in lots of places, but you have never been able to find out who they had belonged to. Hold up examples of the various kinds of buttons in the tin. Tell the children that they are going to be detectives trying to find a person but the only clue they have to help them is a button. From this button they have to work out a description of the person who lost it. They need to find this person because they have useful information which could help with inquiries into a crime.

Divide the children into working pairs. Share out the buttons into the smaller boxes or baskets and give one box to each pair. Allow the children a few minutes to examine the buttons and then ask them to pick out the button they want to use as their clue. Tell the children that they have to examine the button carefully and think about what kind of garment it has come from. When they have come up with two or three suggestions ask the children to decide which one seems to match the button best. When they have decided on the garment, they should try to think of the kind of person who would have worn it and draw a picture of this person wearing the garment. At the bottom of the picture they should write a 'wanted' description of the person, giving detailed descriptions of what the person is wearing and what he or she looks like. The children can take it in turns to write and to suggest descriptions and words.

When the children have completed their description, put two pairs together to form a group of four. In turn, each pair should share their description and the other pair should try to work out from the description which button clue started them off.

## 2
## PACKING THE SUITCASE

### Teaching content

What people wear indicates their character.

### What you need

A copy of *Spot Stays Overnight* by Eric Hill (Heinemann, 1990) – this book can be used to introduce the activity but is not essential; packed suitcase, photocopiable page 48, blank labels for name tags, writing and drawing materials.

### What to do

This is an activity that can be introduced to the whole class, but can be done if necessary with one group at a time – possibly at choosing time. If it is suitable for the age group, the story *Spot Stays Overnight* may be used at the start of the lesson to generate discussion of what different people pack to go on holiday and why.

Settle the class and talk to them about what they would pack to go on holiday to a hot place. They will probably suggest things such as swimsuits, shorts, T-shirts, sandals, sunglasses and so on. Tell the children that this morning you found a suitcase. You don't know who it belongs to – it may be one of the teachers, or somebody who works in the school, or someone else. Perhaps the children can help you to decide who the owner is by taking a closer look at the contents.

Display the suitcase in front of the group. Look at the outside and note any distinctive features:

- Does it look well travelled?
- Does it look like a man's or a woman's case?
- Has it any labels or features which could provide any clues as to its ownership?

Open the suitcase slowly with an expression of surprise. Ask a child to pick out one item and show it to the class. Encourage the children to describe the item and speculate how it may reflect the personality, job or interests of the owner of the suitcase. Then ask another child to select another item and so on until the suitcase is almost empty. Each time, ask the children who they think the item of clothing belongs to and why they think that. At the very bottom of the case there could be one item that provides a definitive clue: perhaps a diary, a letter, a book or a passport with the owner's name in it.

Put the children into groups and assign to each group a picture from photocopiable page 48. Ask the children to think about the type of things such a character would pack in their suitcase. They may like to consider the following:

- the age of the character;
- the job/hobbies of the character;
- the probable type of holiday or trip such a person would take.

Explain that each group is going to design a suitcase and its contents for their character. Give each child a sheet of paper and allow the children five to ten minutes to draw at least four items that this person would pack. (You may want to specify that at least three items must be items of clothing.) Then give the groups a short time to share their ideas and to decide on the colour, condition and type of suitcase they will design. For example, will it be smart or scruffy; have labels; will it have wheels or a pull up handle?

When the children have drawn the clothes for their character and designed a suitcase, ask the children to decide on a name and address for this character and to each write a short description of him or her. Finally, encourage the children to read and compare their descriptions before mounting them into a character passport book. The children can then make a name and address tag for their character from the blank labels.

Show the work at together time and see if the rest of the class can match the characters on the photocopiable sheet with the appropriate suitcase.

### Further development

Ask the children to choose a character, which may or may not be the one that they created the suitcase and clothes for previously, and to write a holiday postcard describing where they are and what they are enjoying doing on the holiday. Display the postcards beside the suitcase/character descriptions, along with a notice inviting the children to match the character to their postcards.

## MIRROR IMAGES

### Teaching content

People dress and behave differently. Becoming a character by dressing up, and observing the dress, actions and mannerisms of other characters, will increase awareness of how differences in appearance gives information about characters.

### What you need

Dressing-up clothes (with beads, watches, scarves, hats, ties, glasses, bags, dresses, waistcoats and so on) in a box, suitcase or clothes basket, large mirror, large sheet of paper, writing and drawing materials.

### What to do

Show the children the dressing-up box and tell them that inside are lots of clothes and accessories which belong to very different kinds of people. Open the box and show the children the various clothes and accessories inside.

Tell them to look at the items and to each choose a selection of clothes and accessories, thinking about the type of person who would wear such things. Allow them a few minutes to dress up, and tell them, as they dress, to think about how to 'become' this person: they should think about who this person is, how they would walk, how they would act, and how they would speak. Give the children a few minutes to walk about in character.

Sit the group in a circle and invite each child in turn to walk round and show off his or her character to the group. As the child is walking round ask the others to talk about what kind of person this is and how this person behaves. For the first few children, you may have to ask questions to illustrate the sort of things they could say:

- Why are you walking like that?
- Where are you going?
- What do you feel like?
- What do you see around you and what do you think about it?
- What sort of house do you live in?
- Who is your best friend?

Write what the children say about their characters on a large piece of paper, for example:

JENNY    I'm going to a wedding in my best hat.

KARIM    I'm really old and have to walk slowly to the shop.

With the children still in their dressing-up clothes, put the children into pairs. Tell the children to look closely at their partner and then draw and write a description of the kind of person they think their partner is. They can describe what they are wearing, how that person acts and what they do.

Suggest to the children that they begin with a drawing of the person and then write descriptive words and phrases around the drawing. If the children have not done this before, it may be necessary to model the format for the children, for example: 'an old man, old cloth cap, walking stick, warm jacket, scarf around his neck, slow steps, smiley face, likes to talk to the children'.

Once they have finished, the children can show their drawing and read their description to their partner. The partner can:

- agree with the description or point out any mistakes (for example, 'I'm not smiley, I'm cross and glaring.');
- give additional information (for example, 'These are my very best shiny shoes.');
- suggest helpful words for describing their character.

Emphasise that this sharing process should produce changes or new information to add to the descriptions. When pairs are satisfied with their descriptions, each pair can stand at the front of the group and share their final drawings and descriptions. Ask others in the group to comment on the parts which they think best sums up each character.

When all the children have had a turn, the dressing-up clothes can be put away and the character drawings stapled into a book or displayed for children to refer to in other writing sessions.

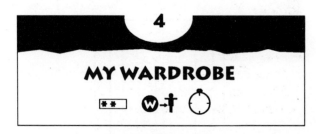

### Teaching content

Characterisation through clothes and appearance.

### What you need

A4 sheets folded (as shown on the next page), clothes catalogues, pictures of clothing from catalogues (cut out without the models showing), photocopiable page 49, scissors, glue, writing and drawing materials.

### What to do

Talk to the children about the different clothes people wear. Their mother and father dress differently from their grandparents, for example.

Show the children the clothes you have cut out of the catalogue. Ask them, 'What sort of person would wear this?' Try to get the children to explain how they know: is it the colour; the style; the type of garment?

Tell the children to pick one member of their family and, using the catalogues, create a wardrobe of clothes for this person. Show them how to cut around the clothes without including any part of the model's face or body. Demonstrate how the folded A4 sheets can be

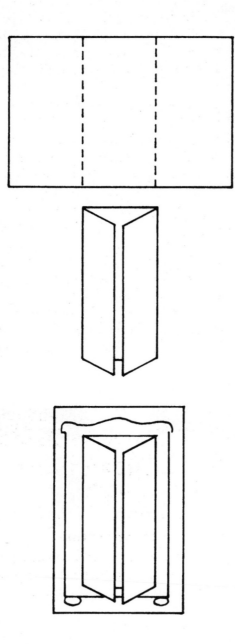

made to open like wardrobe doors and explain that once they have finished these sheets, they can be coloured and mounted on the photocopiable sheet to look like a wardrobe.

Tell the children to write the name of the person whom they have chosen on one of the wardrobe doors. Encourage them to write ages of siblings, if they have chosen brothers or sisters, after the names, or to identify adults, saying whether the person is their mother or father and so on.

When the children have completed the wardrobe sheets, ask them to open their wardrobe 'doors'. Encourage the children to look carefully at each one and guess whose clothes are in the wardrobe, seeking confirmation of this from the child who made it. Afterwards, the work can be mounted on the wall.

## Further development

Use the same activity for fairy-tale characters. Ask the children to draw clothes and select clothes from catalogues to make a wardrobe for characters such as the Ice Queen, The Witch, Goldilocks, The Fairy Godmother, Cinderella, Rumplestiltskin and The Troll.

## 5

# CHOOSING FRIENDS

### Teaching content

Everyone makes judgements and assumptions about people we meet. These may be based on things they do, clothes and appearance, gender and so on.

### What you need

Photocopiable page 50, writing materials.

### What to do

Begin by showing the children the drawings of the characters on photocopiable page 50. Ask the children to look at the pictures and think about them. Which person would they like to meet? Why? Encourage the children to think about how and why they made their decisions. Did they consider how the characters look? How they are dressed? What they are doing? Were there other things that they considered?

Ask the children to consider each person on the photocopiable sheet in turn and to circle those whom they would be very keen to meet and put a cross over those they would not particularly care to meet. If appropriate, the children could also write a brief reason for their decisions on the back of the photocopiable sheet.

Put the children into pairs and ask them to compare their decisions and their reasons. Briefly, take some feedback from the whole class. Encourage the children to consider what they like to know about someone before they decide to be friends, how they get this information, and to ask themselves if it is always reliable – brief impressions can be wrong!

If the photocopiable sheet gives too many examples for younger children to consider, cut out a few of the different characters and enlarge them.

## JUMBLY PICTURES

### Teaching content

An opportunity to create funny or unexpected characters and focus on the detail of their clothes.

### What you need

Photocopiable page 51, chalkboard, scissors, glue, sugar paper (A4 size or slightly larger), stapler, writing and drawing materials.

### What to do

Tell the children that each person in the group is going to draw a different character: a diver, a scarecrow, a clown, a pirate, someone royal, a chef, a witch, a police officer. Either allocate a person to be drawn or let the children choose, and give each child a copy of photocopiable page 51.

Before the children start drawing, tell them to think carefully about what the person does and what kinds of special clothes and accessories they would wear. For example:
• Would the person have something on his or her head?
• What sort of hair/hairstyle would he or she have?
• Would the person wear jewellery or some form of decoration?
• What colour and style of clothes and footwear would he or she have?

Show the children how to draw the head in the top box (joined on to the neck marker on the photocopiable sheet), the body in the middle box (shoulders coming out of the neck marker and ending at the waist), and the legs and feet in the bottom box. Remind the children to use as much space in the boxes as they can to get the proportions correct. It is often helpful to demonstrate this on the board, explaining each stage of the drawing.

Tell the children to think carefully about their character and to include lots of details in their drawings because they are going to use these pictures to make a game. Remind them to include a particular hat or specific facial features, and to make sure that their character is wearing suitable clothes and footwear.

When the children have finished their drawings, tell them to cut carefully along the division lines and to put all the heads in one pile, all the bodies in another and finally all the legs and feet in another. When this has been done, a group leader can deal out the heads, bodies and feet so that each child has a random selection.

Ask the children to reassemble their new character carefully and then to look at it closely and decide who it is, for example 'a queen going diving'. On a separate sheet of paper they should write who the character is, what he or she is wearing and maybe a funny explanation of why the character is dressed like this.

At the end of the activity, place each of the three groups of completed drawings (heads, bodies and legs) on a sheet of A4 sugar paper. Staple on the left-hand side to make a book, in which each page is split into three sections. Each picture is divided at the neck and waist and the children can make their own funny characters by turning the pages of different sections.

## MAGAZINE PICTURES

### Teaching content

Encourages the children to think about a broader range of characters than they often choose to invent in their written stories or play.

### What you need

Magazines, photocopiable page 52, A4 card, scissors, writing and drawing materials.

### What to do

Give out the magazines and ask the children to cut out a picture of a person who they think looks interesting. Do not tell them what they are going to do until they have cut their picture out. Then ask the children to look carefully at the person in their picture and to try to imagine:
• who the person lives with;
• where this person lives and what his or her home looks like;
• what this person's favourite television programme is;
• what sort of pet (if any) he or she owns;
• what this person daydreams about.

For each question, give the children a few moments to think before asking volunteers to share their picture and answers with the class. If the children seem to find this hard, suggest that they show their picture to a child sitting next to them and discuss the question with them, before sharing their pictures and answers with the rest of the class.

Now give each child a copy of photocopiable page 52. Read through the questions and ask the children to write and/or draw their answers in as much detail as possible. Ask each child to stick their magazine picture on to A4 card and to write their name clearly on the back.

### Further development

One week later, give the pictures to different children in the class. Give out copies of photocopiable page 52 and ask the children to consider the questions and then complete the sheet. When they have finished put the pictures on the wall alongside the two photocopiable sheets completed by two different children. Encourage the children to read, compare and discuss each other's answers.

## BUILDING A CHARACTER

### Teaching content

Describing faces; appearances may indicate character.

### What you need

Photocopiable pages 53, 54 and 55, writing and drawing materials, display space.

### What to do

To prepare for this activity, make some spinners from a copy of photocopiable page 53. You will need one for each pair of children. Explain that the children are going to build a character's face and describe it, using a spinner to choose the features of the character's face. Begin by demonstrating to the class what to do.

First show the children the spinner. Point out the features on it. Invite one child to spin the spinner and note the feature that it lands on. Show the children how to refer to photocopiable page 54, which provides a range of different drawings of each feature. Explain that the children must select *one* illustration related to each feature and draw this on to the blank face

on a copy of photocopiable page 55.

Put the children into pairs. Give each pair a spinner and a copy of photocopiable pages 54 and 55. Allow about 20 minutes for them to create their faces. As children finish, display the faces on the wall. When all the children have finished, recall the class and discuss the different faces that the children have drawn. You could begin by asking the children to identify a face you describe. Then ask a child to describe a face and see if the rest of the class can identify it. Encourage the children to use as many different descriptive words as possible. Make the discussion more fun and light-hearted by asking the children to suggest possible personalities for each character: which character looks like a teacher; a burglar; an inventor? Can they find someone who looks angry; happy; contented? Which characters need haircuts? Ensure that the children understand that there is no right or wrong answer to these questions and that everyone's point of view is valid. If appropriate, raise issues to do with how stereotypes based on appearance are not always valid.

Finally, or in a later session, ask each pair to write a short sentence about the character they have created using the following sentence structure:

| My character looks like a . . . . . . . . . . . |
|---|
| because . . . . . . . . . . . . . . . . . . . . |
| . . . . . . . . . . . . . . . . . . . . . . . . |

Older children might like to write a more detailed description, or could develop the idea of challenging the stereotype.

| My character looks like a . . burglar . . . . . . . |
|---|
| because . his eyebrows meet in the middle . . . |
| and his eyes are shifty and small, but really he |
| is a teacher and he likes to do the |
| following things in his spare time . . . . . . . |
| . . . . . . . . . . . . . . . . . . . . . . . . |
| . . . . . . . . . . . . . . . . . . . . . . . . |

Encourage the children to take it in turns to do the writing. Then the work can be mounted and displayed under the appropriate pictures.

### Further development

Orally or on tape, ask the children to describe one of the faces to their partner. Can the partner identify which face it is? Emphasise that clear and accurate descriptions focus on each facial feature in turn and describe it in detail.

# CHARACTERISATION THROUGH SPEECH

## 9

## WHO WILL YOU BE IN STORYLAND TODAY?

### Teaching content
Different characters speak differently and say different things; how they speak depends on who they meet.

### What you need
Photocopiable page 56, marker pens, craft materials for making paper-plate puppet faces (paper plates, wool, pieces of scrap material, coloured paper, felt-tipped pens), chalkboard.

### What to do
Show the children the craft materials and explain that they will be making puppets of characters from stories they have enjoyed. Brainstorm all the different characters they could make: Goldilocks, Big Bad Wolf, Ugly Troll, Baby Bear, Queen, Grumpy, Snow White and so on. Make a list on the board so that children can refer to it.

Choose one character and show the children how to make a puppet, explaining that you are choosing particular materials to highlight different characteristics. After you have made your puppet, ask the children to each pick a character and make a puppet of their own.

Once the puppets have been made, discuss how each character speaks in a different way and says different things. Ask the children to think about the story their character is from and to decide what sort of voice and accent their character has, and what sort of things their character says. Then let the children play with their puppets in small groups, perhaps at free play or choosing time. While the children play, observe and note particular features of their play to facilitate discussion of questions at feedback time.

At feedback time, invite the children to talk about their characters and what they did. Ask them the following questions:
• Who were you today?
• Who did you meet?
• What did you say?
• What were you doing?

Cut out some blank speech bubbles from copies of photocopiable page 56 and write some of the things each character says on the speech bubbles. Make a storyboard display to show the different kinds of things that the characters say and display this near the playing area.

## 10

## WHEN THEY WANT ME TO DO SOMETHING...

### Teaching content
How people speak can tell us important things about them.

### What you need
Photocopiable page 56, a booklet of speech bubbles made from page 56 (with space in-between the speech bubbles for writing), marker pens, chalkboard, display board, Blu-Tack.

### What to do
Tell the class to think about a teacher and their brothers or sisters. Ask the children to think of all the times when these people have asked them to do or not to do something. List the suggestions on the board in two columns: one column for the teacher, and one for the brothers and sisters.

Choose one request from the list on the following page and ask the children to think about the teacher. Have the children ever heard a teacher make a request like this? If so, ask them to try to remember exactly what was said at this time. Encourage the children to try and recall the *exact* words used. If they have not heard a teacher make such a request, encourage them to suggest what the teacher would say and how they would say it.

Write the children's suggestions on to speech bubbles made from copies of photocopiable page 56 and attach these to a display board. Try to get two or three suggestions.

Next, ask the children to think about how a brother or sister would make the same request. Again try to get as many suggestions as possible,

writing each one on to a speech bubble and sticking these on to the display board.

When you have several speech bubbles, stop the activity and review what has been written. Point out the differences between the content and style of the brother or sister's speech and that of the teacher. Explain that brothers and sisters speak in a way that teachers would not. Mix the speech bubbles up. Can the children sort them and tell who the speaker is? Point out that both the words chosen and the content of the request give clues as to who the speaker is.

If necessary, repeat this activity with another situation from the list below. How would each of the chosen groups ask:
• for the television to be made louder/quieter?
• for help to find a missing book?
• for a little less noise?
• for help with carrying something?
• to borrow a pencil?

Choose another situation from the list. Ask the children to work in pairs. Give each pair a speech bubble cut out from a copy of photocopiable page 56 and ask them to write on it what *either* the teacher or a brother or sister would say.

Read some of the children's work out to the rest of the class. Can the children guess who was talking? Display the speech bubbles on the wall.

Finally, show the children the book of speech bubbles you have made. Explain that you are leaving this book of blank speech bubbles

below the display of work from today. Tell the class to listen carefully to the speech of teachers and that of their brothers or sisters over the next few days. If they hear anything that has not already been suggested, they should write it in the book, along with a sentence to describe who the speaker is and, if necessary, the situation.

### Further development
Try making class books of things that, for example, grandparents, parents, football coaches and headteachers would say.

## THE THINGS THEY SAY

### Teaching content
Developing an ear for the speech and language children hear around them.

### What you need
Writing materials (including thick marker pens), large strips of paper, chalkboard.

### What to do
Ask the class whether they have ever noticed that some people always seem to say the same things, or to use the same phrases, over and over again. They may be able to suggest lots of examples but, if not, prompt their thinking by asking if they have noticed what you often say in the situations listed below. What do you say:
• to get the attention of the class/individual children?
• to praise good work?
• to show you are not pleased or are getting impatient?
Write the phrases the children suggest as a list on the board.

Now ask the class to think about their mothers, fathers, brothers, sisters, grandparents or classmates. Ask the children to work in pairs. Tell each pair to choose one person and then write down a list of the phrases that are typical of that person. It may be helpful to prompt their memory by asking questions. You can start with those mentioned above, but others may also be appropriate, such as: 'What does _____ say when:
• you are ill?
• upset?

- have been particularly good/naughty?
- when she or he is tired?
- pleased?
- angry?
- kept waiting?
- looking forward to something?

Try to encourage each child to write a list of about five or six phrases.

Once it is finished, this work can be used in several ways:

*Individual work (easy):* Tell the children to each pick *one* phrase that is particularly typical and to write it on to a large strip of paper. Display these together on the wall under the heading 'Things our _____'s says'.

*Individual work (harder):* Tell the children to put their phrases into the best sequence and write them out, one under the other, to make a list poem called: 'Things my _____ says'.

*Pairs work (middling):* Tell the children to pick two or three phrases from their list and then put them to work with a different pair. Tell each group to combine their lines and decide on the best sequence, thus making a collaborative list poem of between four to six lines.

### Further development

Read the children some of the *Funnybones* books by the Ahlbergs. Part of the big skeleton's characterisation and appeal is his constant use of the phrase 'Good idea'.

# 12

# THINGS I HEAR

### Teaching content

People speak differently in different situations.

### What you need

Enlarged copy (A3 size) of photocopiable anthology page 57, large strips of paper; chalkboard, writing materials.

### What to do

This activity raises children's awareness of different speech patterns and registers. It helps the children to develop an ear for, and an interest in, the language they hear around them.

Show the class the enlarged copy of photocopiable anthology page 57 and ask the children to suggest what sort of person the referee is, and how they know. Generally encourage the children to consider how different people speak and what it is about their speech patterns that tells us about them. The children should appreciate that when we hear *exactly* what someone says, we are better able to draw firm conclusions about them.

Ask the children to think about some of the things that they hear people say at playtime. It may be things that children say to other children or to teachers, or things that teachers say to children. List these on the board. Encourage the children to recall, and make sure that you write down *exactly* what is said. Do not be tempted to paraphrase or reword it.

Now ask the children to repeat what they have just done, but this time to think of things they hear spoken in the classroom. Again, it may be things children say to other children or to teachers, or things that teachers say to children or the whole class. Write this as a separate list on the board.

Give each child *one* thing from the lists to write on to a strip of paper using thick marker pens. Make the children's work into a wall display. You can either sort the display into two headings, or muddle them up and ask people to guess where they were said – at playtime or in class time.

Finally, tell the children that tomorrow you will be asking them to suggest things that people say before school. Tomorrow morning they should listen and try to remember exactly what they heard.

### Further development

The same activity can be done for other times of the school day: things I hear in the morning; at lunchtime; at home time. Or for other places – for example, things I hear at home; at the swimming baths; in the adventure playground.

## WHO WILL YOU BE TODAY?

### Teaching content
By using different props we can be different people and we can speak and act in different ways.

### What you need
Three boxes containing: hats, shoes, bits and pieces. A mirror.

### What to do
Explain that in the dressing-up area today there is a box with hats, a box with shoes and a box with bits and pieces, for example jewellery, scarves, glasses and so on. Tell the children that there is also a mirror, so that they can see themselves 'dressed up'.

Your role in this activity is to observe their play 'in character'. Note how they have dressed, any mannerisms they take on and what they say. The grid below may help in your observations.

|  | What did they put on? | Mannerisms and actions | Dialogue with other children |
|---|---|---|---|
| Child A |  |  |  |
| Child B |  |  |  |
| Child C |  |  |  |
| Child D |  |  |  |
| Child E |  |  |  |

At the end of the session, ask the group to come to the gathering area, or join with the whole class, and remain in their dressing-up clothes. Ask each child in turn to tell the others who they are today, what they did, who they met and what they said.

If the opportunity arises, encourage two children who *did* 'meet' to repeat their dialogue to the class. Draw on your observations to ask further questions and draw children's attention to the different appearances and different voices in the 'characters'.

When each child has had a turn, ask if they would like to become the same person again on another occasion or prefer to be someone else. Try to encourage reasons for their decisions.

Finish the session by returning the props to the correct boxes.

### Further development
You may find the following books useful:
*Two Shoes, New Shoes*, S. Hughes (1986) Hodder & Stoughton
*Sari Games*, Naina Gandhi (1990) André Deutsch

## MISSING MY FRIEND

### Teaching content
Personal qualities and characteristics are as important as appearance.

### What you need
Caption: 'friends'; large strips of paper and marker pens.

### What to do
Tell the children to think about their very best friend, either from school or from home, and to imagine that their friend is moving away so they will not be able to see them every day. Ask the children to think about what they would miss most about their friend.
• Would it be something their friend says when they meet or when they are playing?
• Would it be their suggestions for games to

play or things to do?
• Would it be something funny that only their friend does?
• Would it be something their friend does to help them, or something else?

Ask the children to decide on three different things they would miss about their friend and to write each one on a separate strip of paper, large enough to be displayed on the wall.

Display all the children's contributions in a wheel shape around the word 'friends'. When the wheel is complete, it will read as a circular list of attributes friends can have. Children can read these, and come to recognise the wide variety of different ways in which friends and friendship can be described.

## 15

# I'M A GOOD CHARACTER!

▨ ⬛⬛⬛⬛ ⓦ→🕈 ⭕

### Teaching content
Everyone is different; people can have different views of the same person.

### What you need
Photocopiable page 58; people willing to complete it at home, writing and drawing materials.

### What to do
Children are often not aware of themselves as characters with an individual and unique combination of strengths and talents. This activity helps make them more aware of this.

Talk to the class about the individual talents they have. Some children are very good at doing particular things; some are kind, thoughtful; some are fun; some are quick thinkers, level-headed, organised, reliable or hard-working.

Ask the children to suggest the main (good) characteristic of some of their classmates, and of themselves. Then ask the children what they think other people – their family and friends – would identify as their main good characteristic. Can they guess? Would it be the same characteristic that they have just identified as their own special strength?

Give each child a copy of photocopiable page 58 and read it through with the children. Explain that it must be completed by people they know well. If they don't know their neighbour, for example, they should either leave this section blank, or ask someone else, a family friend perhaps, to complete this part. Explain that they must not tell people what to write. To ensure that children know what to do (and to give the adults an example of what is required), you may help children to complete the first section (friend) in school before they take the form home. The children may draw a picture of themselves in the box provided on the photocopiable sheet.

Once completed, children should bring the sheets back to school, which you can then mount on the wall or display as a class book.

### Further development

Read the children stories with characters who have different individual strengths (and weaknesses):

*Lizzy Dripping*, Helen Cresswell (1974) BBC Books

*My Naughty Little Sister*, D. Edwards (1979) Methuen

*Patch the Pirate Cat*, A. Martyr and P. Lawford (1992) Picture Corgi

*The Trouble with Jack*, S. Hughes (1970) Bodley Head

*Cats of Tiffany Street*, Sarah Hayes (1992) Walker Books

# 16

# GOOD MOODS, BAD MOODS

### Teaching content

Actions to indicate characterisation and mood.

### What you need

Writing materials.

### What to do

Introduce the lesson by reading the children the following extracts.

---

'Dulcie's got it in her this evening,' remarked her mother to her father. 'I'll take her for a spin on the motor bike to blow the cobwebs away.' But Dulcie didn't want to go.

Instead she took a football out into the back garden and practised heading and saving and dribbling and passing to the cat.

'...Dulcie was furious. She was so upset she felt angry spurts of water shoot into her eyes. 'I'll show them...' she muttered to herself, as she kicked an old lemonade can all the way home. 'I'LL SHOW THEM!'

*Dulcie Dando* by Sue Stops (André Deutsch, 1990)

---

But Katie Morag could not and would not get over it. She kept doing naughty things, like stamping her feet and nipping her little brother, Liam.

One day she was so cross that she stomped all the way down to the jetty and kicked her friendly old one-eyed teddy bear into the sea.

'Tiresome Ted!' she shouted, as he disappeared into the choppy waves.

*Katie Morag and the Tiresome Ted* by Mairi Hedderwick (Collins, 1989)

---

Ask the class what sort of mood each character is in and how they know. Do the children ever get in a bad mood? What sort of things do they do? What about when they are in a good mood? What sort of things do they do then?

Compile two class lists: one of things the children do when they are in a good mood, the other of things they do when they are in a bad mood. Some children will volunteer things they say rather than do. It depends on the age of the class whether you accept these – see the 'Further development' activity.

Now ask the children to think about someone else: it might be a member of their family, a friend, neighbour or even a pet! It is important that they choose someone they know well.

Tell the children to use the two starter sentences:

'I know when _____ is in a good mood because...'

'I know when _____ is in a bad mood because...'

Under each sentence, tell them to list all the things this person does that indicates his or her good or bad mood. If one list is much longer than the other, suggest that they observe the person in question for a few days. Later, they may be able to add to their list.

### Further development

The same activity may be done for 'Things I *say* when I am in a bad mood' and 'Things I *say* when I am in a good mood'.

## 17

## BEHIND THE CUPBOARD DOORS

🞮🞮🞮🞮🞮 ⓦ-🕇🕇 ◔

### Teaching content
Environments indicate character.

### What you need
Photocopiable page 59, chalkboard, writing materials.

### What to do
Ask the children to imagine their toy cupboard at home (or the place where they keep most of their toys) and to describe what it is like inside. Do they stuff everything in, higgledy-piggledy so that they can never find anything? Maybe their cupboard is really tidy and organised with everything labelled and in its place? Or perhaps their cupboard is between these two extremes – they can find some things, but there are pockets of chaos – things are supposed to be in the right place, but frequently are not.

Discuss whether the children think that the state of their toy cupboard indicates their personality in any way. Choose one child who is confident and outgoing. Ask the class to guess whether they think this child's toy cupboard is neat and tidy, messy and chaotic or in between. Why do they make the decision they do? Can they guess correctly?

Take a quick show of hands from the class to indicate how many children simply can't abide mess and have to have everything neat and tidy, how many can't stand things being too tidy and are quite able to live in chaos, and how many are in between – is this because they like it tidy, but can't always be bothered, because they quite like clutter, or because they are really messy, but live with a very tidy adult or sibling?

Give each child a copy of photocopiable page 59 and ask the children to discuss which of the people pictured own each of the cupboards shown on the page. Do they agree? Why? When the children have agreed on one character for each of the cupboards pictured, ask them to decide on a name for this character.

Then, tell the children to take one cupboard each and write a short description of the character who they think owns the cupboard. (If the children are very young, you may want to scribe this as a whole class/group activity.) If the children are writing themselves, the following prompt questions on the board may help them to focus their description:
• What does the person look like?

- What clothes is he or she wearing?
- What sort of hairstyle does the person have?
- What sort of things would he or she like doing?

### Further development
Ask the children to each draw their own cupboard at home, with the doors open, and to write a short description of what it is like and what this shows about themselves.

## 18
## CURIOUS CREATURES

### Teaching content
Habitat and environment can influence physical characteristics and personality.

### What you need
Photocopiable page 60, modelling materials, paint, fabric, buttons, writing and drawing materials. Camera (optional).

### What to do
Gather the children together as a class and read them the script below.

---

As the north wind blew softly across the plain there was heard a great gnashing of teeth, scratching of claws and a screeching to chill the blood of those who heard it... as the boulder slowly moved aside, the creatures began their search for another home.

It was dark and lonely here, with only a little light shining through. Strange sounds could be heard, whistling, screeching and rustling. What could it be? What is outside the den?

Strange colours and shapes were all around, moving slowly in the wind. It was amazing to see such other living objects. Little creatures ran around freely. Larger animals were either eating or sleeping. Each creature had been created from different textures; scales shimmered, rugged skin scraped, and fur moved slowly in the gentle breeze.

As the creatures gained in power, the humans began to cover themselves in guises of all shapes and colours. The human face shone out like a beacon to the animals. As a last resort, they took to creating a mask to hide their identity.

---

Ask the children to think about the imaginary creatures that live in such a place. What do they look like? What shape are they? How many eyes, noses, ears do they have? Is their skin furry, smooth, scaly or rough? Do they have horns, antennae, tails, square teeth, sharp teeth or no teeth at all? What noises do they make? Are they shy or bold with humans? Which animals do they like? Which animals do they fear?

Give each table a selection of junk modelling material and ask the children to make their creatures. Once these have been made, put the children into groups of three and tell them to describe their creatures to each other.

Now explain that they will make a passport for each creature. Give each child a copy of photocopiable page 60 and read through the questions. If possible, take a photograph of each creature for the front of the passport (and cut it to size) but, if not, ask the children to draw their creature in the appropriate place.

## 19
## WALLPAPER

### Teaching content
Characterisation through environment.

### What you need
Wallpaper books, photocopiable page 61, chalkboard, scissors, glue, writing materials.

### What to do
Give out the wallpaper books and let the children spend some time looking through the patterns.

Ask the children to choose a wallpaper pattern that would be appropriate for themselves and to say why. Then, ask them to choose a pattern that would be appropriate for their mum. Again, ask why. Establish that people like different types of wallpaper and that often this reflects their age, personality, gender and interests.

Give each child a copy of photocopiable page 61 and tell the children to imagine that the family on the photocopiable sheet are decorating a new house. Each person has been told that they can decorate one room. Ask the children to look through the wallpaper books and decide which wallpaper pattern each person would choose and why. (If they like, they can imagine that they are redecorating their own house, but they may have to invent a few brothers/sisters and grandparents.) As they decide on each wallpaper pattern, they should cut a small sample square and stick it on the photocopiable sheet beside the appropriate person. They can then write the name of each person (real or invented) on the sheet. Ask the children to write on a separate piece of paper about the reasons for their choices. Provide some key words on the board to help them.

## GIFTS

### Teaching content
Characterisation through objects people like and choose to have around them.

### What you need
Catalogues, photocopiable page 62, scissors, glue, writing materials.

### What to do
Talk to the children about how different people like different things. A good present for a six-year-old football enthusiast may not be suitable for a granny or grandpa, or for a child who prefers sewing. The art of buying perfect presents is to think carefully about who the present is for and the sort of things this person admires, needs and likes to do.

Show the children the catalogues. Tell them to imagine that they can buy *one* gift from it for each member of their family or household, up to a maximum of four people. Emphasise that they may only choose *one* gift for each person, so they must think carefully and should be able to explain why their choice is particularly suitable. When the children have chosen their gifts, tell them to cut out each picture.

Give each child a copy of photocopiable page 62. Explain that they may stick one of their gifts on each of the four boxes, writing below each picture who they would buy it for and why this person would like it or need it, for example, 'This is for my mum because she always likes to smell nice.' (Children from families of more than four people can use the back of the sheet also.)

### Teaching content
Different people have different accessories, which can indicate their gender, interests and character.

### What you need
Photocopiable page 63, scissors, glue, writing and drawing materials, schoolbag packed with objects that indicate who it belongs to.

### What to do
Begin the lesson by showing the class the schoolbag you have brought in. Ask the children to consider first the bag itself: Who might it belong to? How can they tell? Then open the bag and begin to unpack it. As you bring out each object, ask them who they now think the bag belongs to, and why?

Ask the children to think about their own schoolbag. If they were to lose it, would the police know that it belonged to someone of their age, sex and interests? If so, how? Children with older or younger brothers or sisters may like to talk about how their own bags differ from those of their siblings.

Give each child a copy of photocopiable page 63 and a blank sheet of paper. Tell them to think of a friend in the class and to write this friend's name on the top of the sheet of paper, with their own name in brackets beside it.

Ask the children to consider the various bags pictured on the photocopiable sheet and to cut out the bag that their friend would be most likely to own. This should be coloured appropriately and then stuck onto the blank paper below their friend's name.

Now tell the children to look at the other items on the sheet. Tell them to choose the *six* items that they think would be in their friend's bag. These should be coloured, cut out and glued on to the sheet.

At together time, children could be encouraged to share, explain and compare their choices. It is good fun to ask the actual children to make choices and then compare the predicted choices with the real thing!

## 22

## MAGIC GLOVES

### Teaching content

Inventing imaginary characters. The things they say, and the clothes imaginary characters wear, can indicate important things about what these characters are like.

### What you need

Photocopiable page 64, selection of glittery and shiny material strips, buttons, cards and fluorescent markers for making motifs, A4 sheets folded into thirds to make a zigzag book, glue, scissors, writing materials (including fluorescent pens).

### What to do

Tell the children to imagine that they own a special pair of magic gloves which give the wearer magical powers. Explain that they are going to make this pair of gloves. Give each child a copy of photocopiable page 64 and ask the children to think about what their magical gloves could look like.

Show the children the resources and let them choose some pieces to decorate their gloves with. They may want to lay these on to the gloves before pasting them on so that they can see what they look like. While the children work, ask them to think about the magical powers their gloves impart and how someone might use such powers. Tell the children that when people have magical powers they may use magic words, have a different name, their voices may change in tone and their appearance may also alter.

When the gloves are ready, ask the children to cut them out and imagine that they are going to wear them. Tell the children to close their eyes and think about what happens to them when they wear the gloves. What are the three special magical powers the gloves give them? Give the children an opportunity to talk to their friends and neighbours about their gloves

Now give the children the zigzag books and ask them to write the name of their magic character across the top of the cover page. They can use fluorescent pens and capital letters if they wish. On the cover they should also draw a picture of themselves wearing their gloves and working their magic. Remind them that if their appearance has changed they should show this in the drawing. At the bottom in small writing they should write their own name.

On each of the pages the children should draw a picture of themselves using one of their magic powers, describing the magic power and

what they are doing at the bottom of each page. If they use magic words they could write these in a speech bubble which could then be pasted on to the finished drawing.

Completed books can be displayed in the book corner.

## FIRST IMPRESSIONS

### Teaching content
First impressions may sometimes indicate character, but not always!

### What you need
Chalkboard, writing materials.

### What to do
Ask the children to choose one of their friends to think about. Can they remember the first time they met their friend?
• Where were they?
• What were they doing?
• What was their first impression? Did they expect to end up friends?

Ask the children to write about their first impressions of their friend. Starter sentences on the board may help some children:

I first saw . . . . . . . . . . . . . .

at . . . . . . . . . . . . . . . . . . . . . . .

She/he was . . . . . . . . . . . . . . . .

When I first saw her/him I thought . . . . . .

. . . . . . . . . . . . . . . . . . . . . . . .

because . . . . . . . . . . . . . . . . . .

. . . . . . . . . . . . . . . . . . . . . . . .

Now I know . . . . . . . . . . . . . . .

. . . . . . . . . . . . . . . . . . . . . . . .

Publish the children's work as a class friendship book. Maybe you could include some of the other activities on friends in this chapter.

## THE NAME SAYS IT ALL

### Teaching content
The name of a character often indicates roles or personality.

### What you need
Photocopiable page 65, labels, Blu-Tack, writing materials. Enlarged copy of photocopiable page 65 for the extension activity.

### What to do
Give each child a copy of photocopiable page 65, which shows six characters and a list of names. Consider the first character (a witch). Tell the children that this is a character in a story and ask them to suggest what the character may be like. Would this person be a hero or a villain? Now read through the list of names in the middle of the sheet, explaining that these

names were suggested by some other children who had also seen the character's picture. Ask the class to suggest which name is the best for this character and why.

Now put the children into pairs and ask them to decide which of the list of names they think is best for the other characters on the sheet and why. Tell them to take each of the remaining characters in turn, to read the list of suggested names and draw a line to connect the name with the character that they agree is best suited to such a name. Tell them to do this for all the characters except the final one (the princess). When the children have done all but the final character, stop the class and ask them to share their answers and the reasons for them.

Then, ask them to consider, in pairs, the final character. They must discuss what the character is like and suggest *one* name for this character, writing it in the space provided. Finally, distribute some felt-tipped pens and the labels, asking each pair to write their own invented name on the label. Attach all labels on the board with Blu-Tack for the class to read. Read through all the names that have been suggested for this character. Why/how did the children choose particular names? Which names do the children think are particularly good? Why?

Take particular care to delight in the character names invented by the children, encouraging them to share their interpretations of the character, how this was reflected in the name and where they got the ideas from for names.

### Further development
Ask each pair to copy–write a label showing their preferred name for each character on the sheet, recording their own names in pencil in smaller writing at the bottom of each label. Use the labels either to make a bar graph to show the class's preferred name for each character, or to display around pictures of each character, cut out from an enlarged copy of photocopiable page 65.

25

## SPECIAL PEOPLE

### Teaching content
Characterisation through action, speech and appearance.

### What you need
Photocopiable page 66, writing and drawing materials, craft materials.

### What to do
Begin the lesson by asking the children to close their eyes and think of someone who is special to them. Ask a few children if they wouldn't mind telling the class who they were thinking of and why. What is it that makes that person special?

Explain that everyone is different. When we like someone very much we appreciate the things that make them different – the way they look, their choice of clothes, the things they say and the things they do.

Ask the children to think about their special person. Can they tell you *one* thing that this person says? It might be something they say to the child, or it might just be an expression they use frequently that the child likes to hear. Take some examples from the class.

Now ask the children to think about the clothes that they love to see their special person wearing. Again, ask some children to share a few examples with the class. Now ask the children to think of the things this person does that makes them special. Again, explain that it may be something quite small – a smile or wave while the child is playing, a hug when they are upset, or a hot drink when the child is cold.

Finally, ask the children to think of *one* thing they like about their special person's face or hair. Take examples, encouraging children to say what it is and why they think it makes their person different.

Give each child a copy of photocopiable page 66 and explain that this will be given as a present to the person whom they have been thinking about. Explain that they should draw a picture of the person at the top of the sheet and write one or two things about the person in each section.

When the sheet is finished, the border of the page could be carefully decorated with various colours, patterns, shiny sequins and glitter. The sheet may then be rolled up and tied with a special ribbon, and a label addressed to the person concerned. The writing can be given as presents for special occasions such as Christmas, Hanukkah, Mother's Day or Father's Day.

## PEOPLE IN OUR SCHOOL

### Teaching content
Observing aspects of characterisation in real life and using these aspects in stories.

### What you need
Blank book entitled 'Our Book of the School', photographs of key people (if required), writing and drawing materials.

### What to do
Introduce the idea of a book about people in the school by explaining that many visitors and children new to the school do not know who works in it, what they do or what they are like. Suggest that it would be a good idea for the children to make a book about all the people who work in the school. It could have pictures or photographs of key people, information about what they do, the sort of things they say, and what pleases them or makes them cross.

Put the children into working pairs and allocate each pair *one* person to write about. If you are using photographs, give them a

photograph of the person. If not, begin the activity by asking the children to do a portrait of the person and to write a short description of what they look like and the clothes they like to wear.

Arrange for the children to find out, either by asking or simply by watching the person closely, what they do, what they say and what they like and dislike. Each pair should do some writing and some drawing about the person, taking it in turns to write and draw.

When the work has been completed, compile a class book which can be displayed in the entrance hall, for instance, or the headteacher's office or the classroom. The following people could be included: the headteacher, teachers, caretaker, cleaner, cook, dinner person, a local police officer, a health visitor, a governor, the school crossing patrol, classroom assistants, parent helpers and children.

# PACKING THE SUITCASE

Scholastic
IMAGINATIVE WRITING
Workshop

# MY WARDROBE

# CHOOSING FRIENDS

Scholastic
IMAGINATIVE WRITING
Workshop

# JUMBLY PICTURES

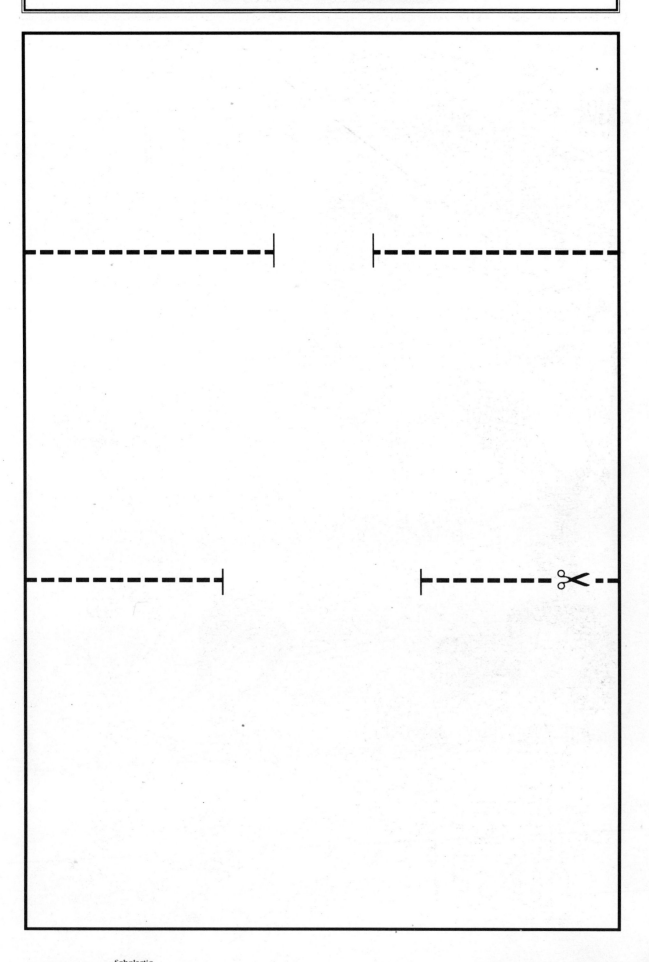

# MAGAZINE PICTURES

This person lives with...

This person lives in...

This person's favourite television programme is...

This person's pet is...

This person daydreams about...

# BUILDING A CHARACTER

Insert pencil into centre hole

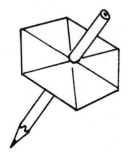

eyes

eyebrow

ears

hair

mouth

nose

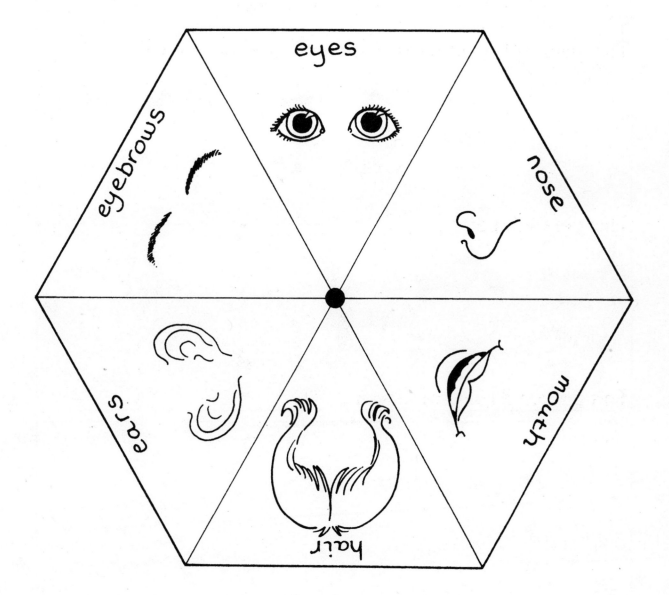

# BUILDING A CHARACTER

nose

eyes

eyebrows

hair

mouth

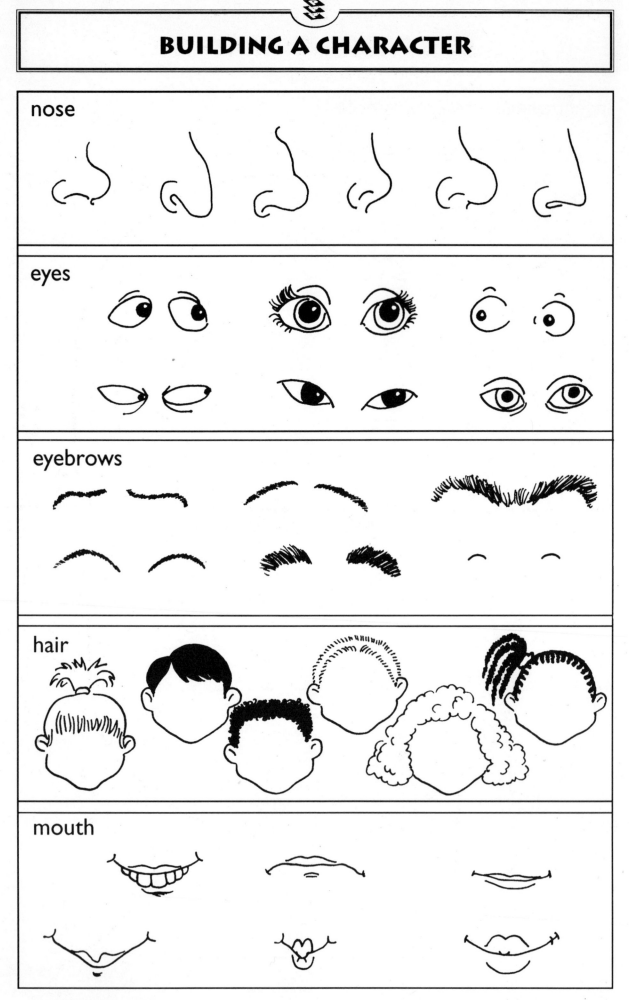

# BUILDING A CHARACTER

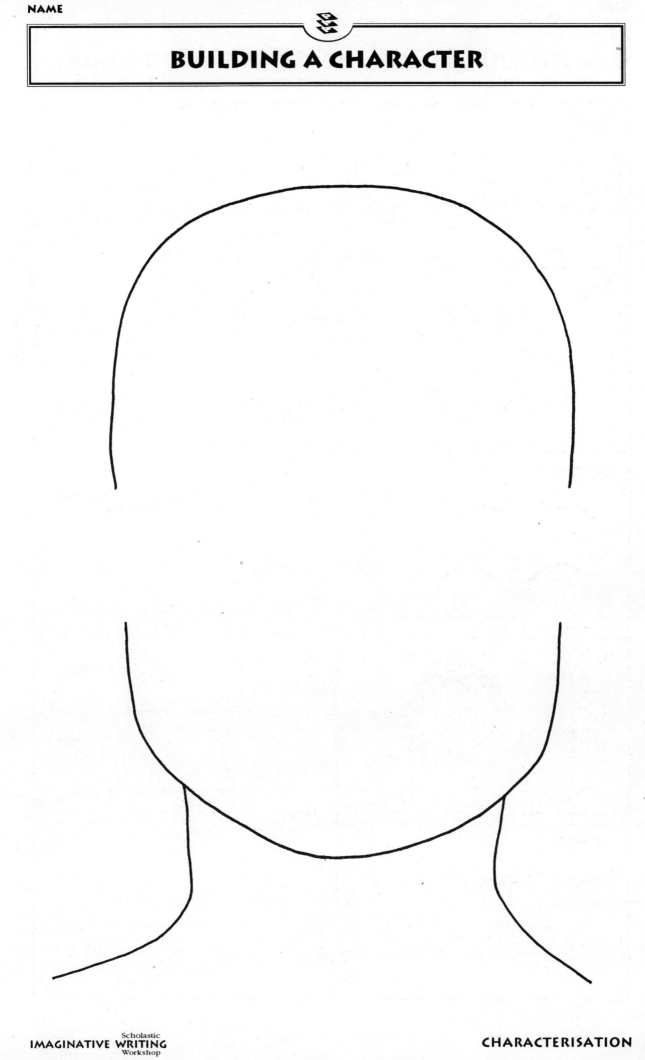

# WHO WILL YOU BE IN STORYLAND TODAY?

# THINGS I HEAR

You shouldn't do that Fred. It says in my book of football rules that kicking other players is wrong. And my dad says players get their names taken for that. Or get sent off. My Uncle Jim was sent off once but that was for calling the linesman a rude word. My Auntie Annie says he calls her that all the time and she never sends him off. Anyway...

# I'M A GOOD CHARACTER!

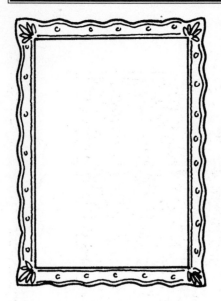 **Good things people say about:**

_____

Please think hard about this person and write down their best characteristic. Please write clearly and, when you have finished, read what you have written to the child.

Friend:

Mum/Dad:

Other relative (brother, sister, grandparents...):

Neighbour:

# BEHIND THE CUPBOARD DOORS

# CURIOUS CREATURES

## Passport for _____

Name:

Place and date of birth:

Nationality:

Family:

Distinguishing features or marks:

Places visited:

# WALLPAPER

# GIFTS

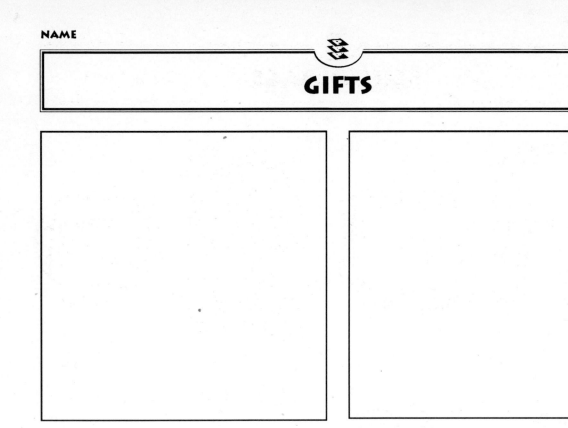

This is for _____

because

This is for _____

because

This is for _____

because

This is for _____

because

# SCHOOLBAGS

# MAGIC GLOVES

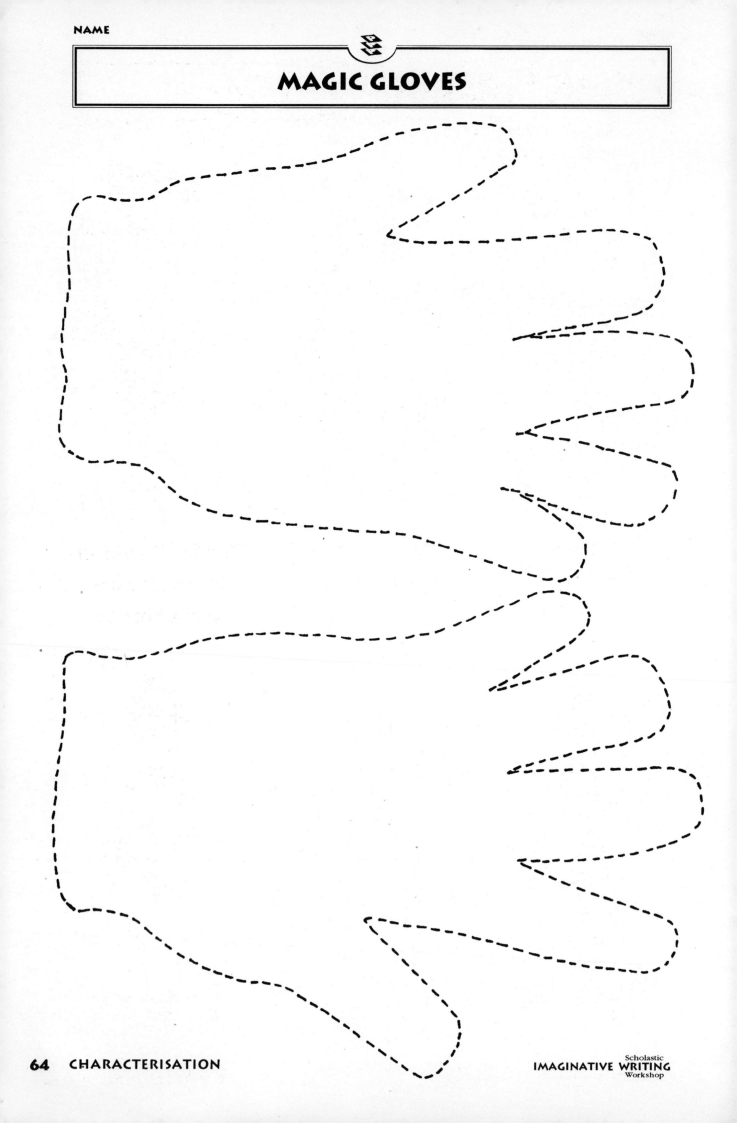

Scholastic
**IMAGINATIVE WRITING**
Workshop

# THE NAME SAYS IT ALL

Sluggy Wuggy
Whoopy May
Griselda Grime

Mrs Salterpot
Annabel Smart
Joy Dumperton

Winnie Wichester
Doris Drudge
Serena Shadow

# SPECIAL PEOPLE

You're special because you say...

You're special because you wear...

You do special things...

You look special...

*Chapter Four*

# PLACE AND SETTING

# INTRODUCTION

## Why is setting important?

Setting provides the backdrop against which characters come to life and tell their stories. The physical setting and a sense of time are important, but the way in which a writer sets the scene for a story can tell the reader far more than where and when the story takes place.

> Once upon a time there was a dark, dark moor. On the moor there was a dark dark wood...

This opening sentence from *A Dark, Dark Tale* by Ruth Brown tells the reader where the action takes place – the physical setting – but also establishes the mood and atmosphere of the story. This helps to locate the story in the reader's imagination and influences what the reader expects. The reader has formed an opinion about what this place and story will be like.

## What do children know about setting?

Children are familiar with their own home settings. They know a lot about these familiar places and what makes them seem like home. Visits to other families will show obvious similarities but will also reveal differences. Children will also be familiar with local scenes, and these will be varied: town life with busy roads, built-up streets, crowds, supermarkets and parks; rural life with scattered communities, fields, lanes and maybe one local shop. Many children will have moved beyond these local settings through holidays and outings.

The ways in which familiar places change depending on the time of day, weather and season will also be part of their knowledge. Some children may also be aware of changes in atmosphere and emotion. A relaxed day out on a shopping trip is very different from a frenetic race round the supermarket.

Children will incorporate these settings in their play. When they dress up to go to the shops they know what these shops should be like. They will often move furnishings and resources around and say: 'This is the supermarket. Let's make this the checkout, and here's the sweet counter.' Or: 'This is the boat from my holidays. You need to have a wheel to make it go.' They know that all the players need to understand the physical landscape if they are to envisage the story.

Children gain an even wider experience of setting through listening to stories. Some of these will connect with settings similar to the children's own. This helps them to identify similarities in detail as well as differences. Traditional and imaginative stories enrich their experience of settings and of the detail within them. For example the witch's oven in *Hansel and Gretel* would be very different from the cooker at home.

Children will have learned that stories happen somewhere, sometime, and may be beginning to differentiate between the mood and atmosphere conveyed by different stories. When they ask for a story by type and describe it in this way, for example: 'We want a scary story. Can we have the *Haunted House* story?' (pop-up book by Jan Pienkowski), they are showing the beginning of awareness of genre. However, they may not be conscious of how writers convey these messages about mood through their descriptions of the setting. Coming to understand that this is what story writers do, and the variety of ways in which this can be done, is as necessary to young writers as being able to give descriptions of the physical features themselves. With young story-makers, the experience of talking about the settings, moods and emotions in stories and the variety of ways in which authors build up these pictures is vital. However, young children's enjoyment of stories is also vital, so it is important that opportunities for talking about setting come after a chance to enjoy the story for its own sake.

Often in story books for young children much of the setting, both in terms of place and mood, is conveyed by the illustrations which accompany the text. Talking about these illustrations in the context of the story is an important way in which children learn about and acquire a vocabulary to describe settings and scenes in stories.

## What do children need to learn?

Children need to learn:
- to notice the details of settings in real life and in stories;
- to describe these physical attributes in ways that help others to see what they have seen;
- that readers and listeners do not share their knowledge of the scene and do not have the same mental picture of the setting or its atmosphere.

Children need to be asked questions which

help them to identify what information others require and which help them to revisit, re-explore and clarify the key components of the setting for themselves. They need wide experience of sharing stories so that they build up a repertoire of different kinds of story setting. They need encouragement to notice and talk about the different ways in which storytellers set the scene in both physical and emotional terms. These messages about setting will be conveyed in the text of the story and in the illustrations. Children need to be encouraged to notice and discuss both the written messages conveying setting and the illustrations of settings, and the links between them. They need to try out these different and complementary strategies themselves and to make judgements about how successful they have been in conveying the type of setting and atmosphere they intended.

Children need time to talk about, consider and compare the different methods they have used to convey settings in their stories. They need frequent opportunities to try out these different ways of setting the scene in short pieces of writing, as well as creating extended contexts for writing.

Young children are often impatient to get to the main action in a piece of writing so they will need encouragement and a variety of practical activities to help them create and relate the setting. They need to be introduced to different ways of creating contexts and settings (through play, drawing, talk and the use of artefacts and resources) for their stories and be encouraged to explore these. Children will have to be reminded of other occasions when writing about settings has been a focus, and encouraged to incorporate what they have learned from previous writing and story experiences.

Devising detailed contexts which detail the settings for their stories requires time, stimulation, support and encouragement.

## How can teachers help?

*Teachers need to provide opportunities for children to explore settings in their play.* Role-play, puppets or small worlds materials (small construction sets, streets, farms, houses and so on) can be useful in helping children to rehearse different ways of creating settings. When children talk about the places they are creating and the details of these scenes and share their ideas with other children, they are developing both a range of settings and identifying what should be included within them. This allows

the teacher to observe what children know and how they explain their ideas about settings. The teacher can join in and talk to the children about how they have created the settings for their play and help the children to identify the key components of them. This is useful for the child at the time, but the teacher can also refer to this in future writing lessons and remind the children about what they had to do in their play and help them to use this in setting the scenes for their stories.

*Teachers need to provide children with a range of story experiences which illustrate a wide variety of settings.* Children need to enjoy these stories for themselves and then, when they have become familiar with the story, can be encouraged to notice how the authors have set the scene. Talking about what the author has written in order to convey the physical and emotional setting, and about the illustrations in the story, will help the children to become conscious of the devices which can be used. In this way, children will gradually begin to experience the story not only as a reader but also to view it with a writer's eye.

Selecting books for the story corner which illustrate effective strategies for creating settings is useful. For example, children can be asked to create their own displays of story books which have a variety of pictures and descriptions of gardens (magic gardens, snowy gardens, flowery gardens, secret gardens, vegetable gardens) and which show how different writers have portrayed both the physical setting and its mood.

*Teachers need to plan writing tasks which focus on setting.* They need to offer opportunities for children to try out different ways of creating settings – sometimes broad pictures of places, sometimes finely detailed, or perhaps looking at a place and considering how it would alter at different times because of the weather, for example, or a change in mood or atmosphere. For young or inexperienced writers this will involve lots of opportunities for talking about setting; opportunities for the creation of settings either in play or in three-dimensional forms and experience of drawing settings.

*Teachers must create situations which involve children in both describing the settings they have created to others and being questioned about these.* This helps children to clarify the detail that the listener requires. What is important is that children can identify methods of creating the settings and understand what is involved in conveying their own picture to another. This is perhaps what is most difficult for young children: recognising that other people don't have the same knowledge of the setting or the same picture in their minds. They need frequent experience of telling someone else about their setting and asking about the settings created by others. By being asked questions about the settings they create, they will realise what it is that readers and listeners need to know in order to picture the setting – which details are required, the sequence of description and the range of words that can be used. Asking questions of others will reinforce this learning. Teachers need to be involved in this to help children to identify and note what they have learned about other viewpoints.

*Teachers must encourage children to see themselves as writers and to put their ideas about place and setting into writing.* Inexperienced writers will need support to do this. Teachers need to model ways of creating settings with children and may also need to model ways of writing about them. Sometimes, the teacher may take over the writing process by scribing, so that children can concentrate on the ideas and words required. On other occasions, children may write together, taking turns to be the writer or to suggest ways of describing settings. This should help children. to become more confident about producing their own written setting descriptions.

*Teachers need to be positive in responding to children's writing about setting.* They need to encourage development not by pointing out what is missing or asking for more detail – which only adds length, induces boredom or creates anxiety – but by asking the children what else the reader would want to know and what would be a good way to tell them. (Will someone reading this know it was a dark night? How will they know it was a happy place?)

# CONTENTS AND ORGANISATION

The activities in this chapter aim to raise children's awareness that stories happen in different places and that as writers they need to learn how to describe them in ways which will convey their intentions to someone else. It also provides activities which will focus children's attention on not only the physical setting but also on the mood, atmosphere or emotion that

a writer wants to convey and ways of doing this. The following aspects are covered through activities in which children invent and describe places and scenes.

## Building vocabulary, detail and structure of description

These activities help children to observe and record descriptions of familiar settings. Talking about their own real-life experiences helps children to recognise both the broad brushstrokes necessary to orientate the readers as well as identifying the key details which need to be included so that they can fully understand. Paired work encourages children to understand someone else's perspective. Writing about such places can help children to experience a familiar setting in a different way. The activities should begin to convey to children that short descriptions using a few well-chosen words are more effective than lengthy, contrived descriptions. For young children, just building up a range of effective description words will be important.

## Creating places

These activities offer children a variety of methods to generate and select ideas for imaginary places. The activities encourage children to draw, talk, play, paint, model and write to firm up their initial ideas. Paired and group work encourages children to draw on previous story experiences and those of others. Again, children are encouraged to invent in detail and to write short descriptions using a few well-chosen words effectively.

## Emotive descriptions

These activities have been designed to give children experience of exploring places not only in physical terms but also through emotions and senses. This will help them to begin to understand the importance of identifying the feelings or atmosphere which settings can evoke and the necessity to convey this to the reader if they want the reader to have a similar emotional response to the story.

## Bibliography – children's books

*A Dark, Dark Tale,* Ruth Brown (1992) Red Fox
*Haunted House,* Jan Pienkowski (1979) Heinemann

| | Activity | Teaching content | Star rating | Group size | Photo-copiable |
|---|---|---|---|---|---|
| 1 | I'm thinking of a place | Places can be described in different ways | */** | 4⇨2 | ✓ |
| 2 | My favourite place | Strategies for creating settings | */** | 4⇨1 | |
| 3 | 'But my school has...' | Detail is important in describing place | */** | 1⇨4 | A |
| 4 | The view from my door | Describing familiar places | */*** | 1 | ✓ |
| 5 | Through the window | Structuring descriptions of a place | **/*** | 2 | |
| 6 | Holiday places | Structuring description of a place | ** | 2 | |
| 7 | Night sounds/morning sounds | Sounds help create the mood of a setting | **/*** | Ⓦ⇨2 | A |
| 8 | The wheels on the bus | Places have specific buildings and features | * | Ⓦ⇨2 | ✓ |
| 9 | The building site | Creating detail and vocabulary for an imaginary setting | * | 4 | |
| 10 | I'm in the classroom but... | Imaginary places need detailed descriptions | ** | Ⓦ⇨1⇨Ⓦ | |
| 11 | Special bedrooms for special people | Using place to depict character | **/*** | 2 | ✓ |
| 12 | Magical mystery tour | Stories can have real or imaginary settings | **/*** | Ⓦ⇨1⇨Ⓦ | ✓ |
| 13 | In a dark, dark wood | Changing the setting through a story | **/*** | 4 | |
| 14 | Watery places | Using sounds to describe imaginary settings | * | Ⓦ⇨1⇨2 | A |
| 15 | Me in different places | Using setting to indicate emotional mood | */*** | Ⓦ⇨1 | |
| 16 | The dark den | Focus on detail in setting to create mood | */*** | 4 | |
| 17 | Autumn leaves | Place can be described through senses and emotions, not just visual detail | */*** | 4 | ✓A |
| 18 | Music dreams | Personal images require detailed description | ** | 1⇨2 | |
| 19 | Place-names | Place names often evoke strong images | **/*** | 4⇨2 | ✓ |
| 20 | Add some detail | Descriptive detail contributes to setting | ** | 1 | ✓ |
| 21 | Daytime/night-time | Settings can create different moods | *** | Ⓦ⇨1 | |
| 22 | Happy places/scary places | Colour, shape and weather create different moods | */** | Ⓦ⇨4⇨2 | ✓ |

A = photocopiable anthology page
Ⓦ = whole group

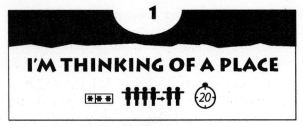

# I'M THINKING OF A PLACE
▣▣▣ 𝍩→𝍬 ⑳

### Teaching content
Places can be described in different ways.

### What you need
Photocopiable page 86, writing materials.

### What to do
Children need to work in pairs for this activity so, before beginning, arrange chairs and tables accordingly so that children working together can listen without difficulty and can have a place to put their cards.

First of all, gather the group together and tell them that they are about to do a task that involves a lot of listening and describing. Tell the children to listen very carefully as you describe a place on the photocopiable sheet in front of you, without naming the place and without letting the children see the picture. It may help if the children close their eyes to concentrate on imagining the scene.

When the children are settled, describe the scene you have chosen from the photocopiable sheet. For example, 'I can see lots of fish here. This is a very peaceful place. Everything looks very blue. There are different-sized rocks and some seaweed is floating above me.' When you have finished, ask the children to open their eyes and guess the place you have depicted. Use this opportunity to talk with them about:
• particular words that helped to orientate them;
• what the 'picture' looked like in their mind;
• words that gave some detail.

Put the children into pairs, and give one copy of photocopiable page 86 to each pair. Explain what the children need to do. Tell them to hold the photocopiable sheet so that both of them can see it. Explain that one child becomes the 'describer' first. Child A chooses a scene and describes it in as much detail as possible without mentioning the place-name. The other child has to listen without speaking and when Child A has finished describing, Child B has to select the picture which depicts the scene described. Then the children swap roles.

Your role in this activity is to listen to the descriptions being given and to observe how the children describe the pictures.

When the children have finished describing and selecting, let them choose one picture from the photocopiable sheet and write down five sentences to describe the scene.

# MY FAVOURITE PLACE
▣▣▣ 𝍩 ㊺ → ⑮

### Teaching content
Settings can be represented using different media to enable children to focus their talk and activity on 'place'.

### What you need
Model-making junk materials, construction kits, play dough, blank labels, camera, writing and painting materials.

### What to do
Due to the nature of this activity, it may be implemented most effectively with a small group, with groups being rotated over a period of time to enable each child to have the opportunity to create a model.

Begin by gathering the small group around you or at a table. Tell the children that you are going to be thinking about your favourite place and making a model or picture of it. Talk about *your* favourite place, what it looks like and why you like it.

Ask the children to turn to the person sitting next to them and talk about their favourite places, what they look like and why they like them. In turn, ask each child to tell the group about a favourite place.

Now tell the children that they can each choose to make a model of their favourite place either with junk materials, construction kits, paint, paper or play dough. Before they rush off to 'create', give the children some thinking time to decide the best media for their model. If appropriate, they could make a plan of what they are going to make. Discuss with individuals any other resources they may need. Your role throughout this session is that of facilitator – talking with the children to help them clarify which details are important, discussing the moods, feelings and memories evoked by the models at each stage of development and supplying and suggesting resources to enhance the detail in the models.

Children will have very different finishing rates, with some even choosing to come back to refine their models at a later time. All models, however, will have to be valued for what they represent to the children. To this end, make a label for each model and put them on display, or take photographs of the labelled models.

Ask the children to write a short description of their favourite place, explaining why it is important to them. The photographs and writing could be displayed on the wall or included in an album for the class library or in a construction area of the classroom.

## 'BUT MY SCHOOL HAS...'

### Teaching content
A place is given its character by its physical features and by the people who inhabit it.

### What you need
Photocopiable anthology page 87, card, collage materials for book cover, chalkboard, writing and drawing materials.

### What to do
Begin by asking the children to describe key features of a school. Give each child a copy of photocopiable anthology page 87 to use as a prompt for ideas. They will probably suggest things which involve the teachers, the physical

environment and what takes place in it. Encourage the class to give you about ten to fifteen suggestions and list these on the board.

Most of the things the children mention will be common to most schools. Tell the children that you are interested in what is special and different about these features in their own school.

Write 'Most school have... (playgrounds)... but MY school playground has...' Ask the children to finish this sentence by saying what it is that distinguishes their playground from others. Encourage as many alternatives as possible and write them on the board.

Now suggest that each child chooses another feature to think about. Tell them to draw a picture of it and below the picture to write, using the structure provided, what it is that makes this different and special.

Once they have finished, put the children into groups to compile their work into a book about their school. You will need to ensure that each group's descriptions contain a variety of different features. Explain that the children have to decide on:
• the best order for the pages in the book – whose work will go first, second, third and so on;
• the best title for the book;
• the best layout and picture for the front cover.

Finally, allow the groups to read each other's books, before displaying them in the school library.

### Further development
This idea can be adapted to different contexts, such as My house, My street, My town. When the children have completed their writing, ask them to read the books in each category and compare them. This will enable them to see the full range of stories created about each place.

Then ask the children to imagine, still with their eyes closed, that they have opened the door and are just about to step out. What do they see? Is there a garden? Pavement? Balcony? Are there railings? Cars? People?

Give each child a copy of photocopiable page 88 and ask the children to draw exactly what they see as they open their door to leave, in the right-hand rectangle when the page is used as a landscape sheet.

Then help them to cut around the door shape on the left side of the sheet. Show them how to fold the paper in half so the door 'opens' to reveal the scene. Let them decorate the outer half of the folded sheet.

Finally, ask the children to write a short description of the scene that they have drawn behind their door.

## THROUGH THE WINDOW
⟦*****⟧ †† ⟨20⟩

### Teaching content

Sometimes we take familiar places for granted and don't notice their detail. This activity gives a strategy to help children to observe and structure detail in their descriptions of a familiar place.

### What you need
A window for looking through, writing materials.

### What to do
Ask the children to work in pairs to make a list of everything they can see from the window. They should start by noticing what is closest to the window and then gradually work out to the middle distance and then as far as the eye can see: for example, in the playground, near the fence, in the street, outside the school. This can be a series of small pictures, a wordlist or a combination of both.

The children should take it in turns to observe, draw and write. At the end, both partners should check that everything has been recorded. The children should then look out of the window again and identify one detail which they had not noticed before and write a short description including what it is, what it looks like, where it is and why it has not been noticed before.

## THE VIEW FROM MY DOOR
⟦****⟧ † ○

### Teaching content
Familiar places are often more difficult to describe because we take them so much for granted.

### What you need
Photocopiable page 88, glue, scissors, writing and drawing materials.

### What to do
Ask the children to close their eyes and imagine that they are ready to leave their house to go to school. They approach the door:
• Is it the front or the back door?
• What does the door look like from the inside?
• Are there hooks or coats hanging on it?
• Does it have a cage for collecting post, or a device for stopping draughts?
• Is there any furniture beside the door, or anything hanging on the walls?

## 6

# HOLIDAY PLACES

### Teaching content
Structuring descriptions of a place.

### What you need
Children will need to each bring in a photograph of a place where they have been on holiday; writing materials.

### What to do
Ask the children to bring in a photograph of themselves, or their family, on holiday. (Explain that a holiday can be a visit to grandparents or friends, a one-day trip or a longer period away from home.) Put the children into pairs and give one child in each pair three minutes to tell their partner all about the place they went to and what it was like. Then swap and let the other halves talk about their holiday place.

Then, ask the children to each list four or five things that made their holiday place different from home. If appropriate, this may be done in pairs.

Finally, show the children how to take each item on the list and expand it into one or two sentences. In this way, the children should end up with five to ten sentences describing their holiday place. Suggest they read these through and number them to show the best order (encourage discussion with partners, if appropriate). Finally, show the children how to frame or mount their photographs, and how to choose an appropriate layout for the text before copying it into a readable form.

When this is displayed, either on the wall or as part of a class or group book, ask the children about the decisions they made on sequence, layout and presentation and why they made those decisions.

## 7

# NIGHT SOUNDS/MORNING SOUNDS

### Teaching content
Sounds are an important detail in describing places and settings.

### What you need
Photocopiable anthology page 89, black paper, yellow paper, card, A4 paper – halved horizontally and then turned sideways for writing, chalkboard, glue, writing materials.

### What to do
Two days before you want to do this writing activity, gather the children together just before they go home and tell them that you want them to find out about the sounds that happen in their house when they are in bed at night-time. Ask them to listen very carefully once they are in bed with their lights off, just before they go to sleep, and to try to remember what they hear. This might be: the sounds of older children or adults, talking, noise from the television, people saying goodnight to each other, someone locking the door and switching the lights off; or it might be the quiet noises the house makes when everyone is settled for the night – floorboards creaking, windows rattling, clocks ticking.

The day before you do the activity, remind the children to listen again. Then, at school, ask the children to make notes of what they heard.

Gather the children together and ask them to tell you what they heard. Make a list of these on the board. Organise the sounds into:
• voices and people activities, for example people brushing their teeth, showering, washing;
• settling-down sounds, for example locking up, switching off the lights;
• quiet house sounds.

Next, ask the children to develop their lists into sentences, writing about their own night-time sounds, starting with the voices and activities they heard, then the settling-down sounds and then the quiet sounds. Give them the final sentences: 'Nothing could be heard now. The whole house was asleep.'

When this activity has been completed, repeat for morning sounds. Talk to the children about waking-up sounds in their house. Ask the children to listen carefully and remember the sounds they heard, from the moment they began to wake up, until everyone was out of bed and getting ready. Give the children the story starter: 'The house started to wake up.'

Ask the children to cut out and paste their night sounds half of the A4 sheet on black paper and their morning sounds section on yellow paper, leaving a border of about 4cms all the way round. Mount both pieces of writing side by side on a larger piece of card for display.

To conclude the activity, give each child a copy of photocopiable anthology page 89. Read the poem about the sounds in a house, 'The sounds in the evening' with the children. Discuss with them the similarities and differences between their descriptions and the writer's description of the sounds in the house in the poem.

### Further development
Similar activities could be done in school, for example classroom sounds, playground sounds, or children could listen to sounds outside at night and sounds outside in the morning.

## 8
# THE WHEELS ON THE BUS

### Teaching content
Different places have specific buildings and features.

### What you need
'The wheels on the bus' song, photocopiable page 90, card, large sheet of paper, zigzag book, writing and drawing materials.

### What to do
Begin by singing the song 'The wheels on the bus' with the whole class. Next, ask the children to suggest the different places the bus might travel through on its journey. Draw on the children's own experiences of bus journeys, but encourage them to extend from the familiar settings of local streets, shops and parks to locations further afield like the seaside, the city, the countryside, the farm or the zoo.

As children make suggestions, list these on a large sheet of paper and point out the variety of places the bus could go to. Then put the children into pairs. Assign a place to each pair and ask them to draw what that place would be like. Before they start, tell them to think about a traveller on the bus and to imagine what the traveller would see through the window. How would the traveller know he or she had arrived at this particular place – what special buildings or features would be visible? Tell them that someone on the bus would have to recognise the place by the details they include. Children can take turns to draw and to suggest ideas.

### Further development
When all the children have finished, collate their pictures in a zigzag book. At the bottom of each page cut slots for inserting the card bus labels. Make the bus labels by photocopying page 90 on to card and cutting out each bus. Write the name of each child's destination in the blank space on the side of each bus, for example 'city centre shops', 'farm' and so on. Place the bus labels in an envelope and attach it to the back cover of the zigzag book. The book can then be displayed in the story corner. Children should try to match the labels to the appropriate places when they choose to look at the drawings in the book.

Scholastic
**IMAGINATIVE WRITING**
Workshop

## 9

### THE BUILDING SITE

■▭ ††††  ⊘20

#### Teaching content
Creating details of an imaginary setting.

#### What you need
Sand tray, wet sand, play people, miniature tools, for example DUPLO or Playmobil sets and construction vehicles, bulldozers, diggers and so on, folded cards for labels, writing materials.

#### What to do
This activity could be done at a free-choice time or could be structured as part of the language programme.

Place the materials in the sand tray and let the children build up the imaginary building-site scene. The resources alone should be sufficient to prompt the development of a building site but you can prompt this with statements and questions: 'That's a big mound of sand. Have you moved it there to let the road be built?'

When the children have had time to construct their scene, begin to talk to them about it. Ask them to explain what this place is and to give details of the scene.

As children explain, write down key words and phrases on small pieces of folded card and insert these at appropriate points in the building-site scene.

Ask the children to write about the scene they have created. Give them a starter sentence: 'Today we made a building site'. Encourage them to use the labels to write a more detailed description of the scene. These can be displayed in the sand area.

When the activity has been completed, an alternative activity to undertake with younger children or inexperienced writers is to leave the labels in place until a suitable point in the day when children can report back on the play and activities they have carried out. Encourage each child to explain part of the scene, using the labels to remind them of key points.

## 10

### I'M IN THE CLASSROOM BUT...

■■▭  ⓦ→†→ⓦ  ⊘25

#### Teaching content
Imaginary places can be described in as much detail as real places. People imagine places in different ways.

#### What you need
Writing and drawing materials.

#### What to do
With the children gathered around you, begin by asking them to close their eyes and think of a place they would like to be if they were not in the classroom. You might suggest one or several places: for example, in the jungle, up a mountain, above the clouds, under the sea, at the top of the beanstalk, at the door of the castle, in a magic wood.

With their eyes still closed, ask the children:
• What does the place look like?
• Can you see colours in your place?
• Is it big/busy/quiet/noisy?
• Are there any people, animals, objects?
Tell the children to open their eyes and

'hold' on to this picture, and without talking to anyone to go back to their seats. Ask the children to draw their place in as much detail as possible, remembering all that they saw. When they have finished, tell the children that they will now describe the place they imagined, in writing. They should complete the story start: 'I'm in the classroom but...' Discuss as a class the variety of places drawn and ask the children to suggest useful words to describe the places.

The drawings and descriptions could be displayed in a writer's area with labels in bold print for place settings and descriptive words.

### Further development
Pair the children with someone who drew a similar place. Ask them to take turns to describe their place to one another and to compare their pictures and descriptions. Ask them to find three things which were different in their partner's picture and description from their own.

## SPECIAL BEDROOMS FOR SPECIAL PEOPLE

### Teaching content
Description of place; using place to depict character.

### What you need
Photocopiable page 91 enlarged to A3 size, A3 paper, writing and drawing materials.

### What to do
Begin by showing the children photocopiable page 91. Explain that it is the bedroom of a fairy-tale character. Whose do they think it might be? (It is a picture of Cinderella's bedroom.) Go through the evidence systematically: the ragged clothes, the old dressing table, the worn books, the frayed bedspread, the broom, the photographs on the walls (of the ugly sisters).

Ask the children to work with a friend to draw and describe the bedrooms of other fictional characters. They may choose from a list you provide (for example, a prince or princess, a robot, a mad scientist, an elf, a knight, a pirate, a wicked stepmother, a good fairy) or suggest their own.

Give each pair an A3 sheet of paper for this drawing. Explain that they must decide together whose bedroom they are drawing and what that bedroom will look like. Tell them that they will need to discuss what will be in it and where it will be, before deciding who will draw what.

Remind the children that discussion and negotiation are very important – you do not want two beds, two dressing tables and so on. Stress that they should help each other with ideas and that they should make sure that the final drawing fills the sheet, which means that individual objects need to be of a decent size!

Once finished, ask each pair to describe their drawing to the class or to the other people on their table. Then, ask them to write a short piece describing who lives in the room and what it is like. Finally, ask them to write about two things in the room that are particularly precious to its occupant and why. Explain that the pairs should work together on the writing and take it in turns, perhaps writing one sentence each. The child who is not writing should help by providing ideas, words and spellings.

The work can be made into a 'big book' entitled 'Who lives here?'

## MAGICAL MYSTERY TOUR

### Teaching content:
Stories can be set in many places, both real and imaginary.

### What you need
The story of *Aladdin*, photocopiable page 92, display board, scissors, writing and drawing materials.

### What to do
Many children are familiar with the story of *Aladdin*, and in particular with the character of the Genie who grants wishes. Begin by recalling the story or reading the part of the story where the Genie asks Aladdin what his wishes will be.

Ask the children to close their eyes and imagine that the Genie has just told them that they can go to any two places they want to. Ask them 'Where would be the places you would most want to go and why?' When the children have had a few moments to think, ask them for some suggestions, encouraging good ideas and noting the variety of places.

Give each child a copy of photocopiable page 92 with the two 'dream clouds'. Ask the children to draw a picture of two favourite places they have imagined and to label them 1 and 2 in order of priority.

As the children are doing this, look at their pictures to gauge the most popular places. When they have finished drawing, ask the children to cut out carefully around their dream clouds. Gather the whole class back together again and select one place which you have noted as popular. Ask how many have chosen this as a first or second choice, and attach these to the display board.

Continue to collate the children's responses until a frieze has been built up with a variety of drawings of dream clouds.

Use the frieze to ask:
- Why do you think... is the most popular?
- What kinds of things would you be able to do there?
- How many of the places are real/imaginary?
- Which places are near/far away?

Later, display these in a more fixed position and label the groups of dream clouds accordingly. Ask the children to suggest a title for the frieze.

### Further development

Extend this activity by asking the children to write about what they would do if they journeyed to their dream place. Children's writing could then be added to the frieze.

## 13

# IN A DARK, DARK WOOD

⬛⬛⬛⬛⬛ 𝍏 ㉚

### Teaching content

Some settings change from a large space to much smaller places and spaces.

### What you need

*The Dark, Dark Wood* (traditional tale, published by Story Chest), blank A5 cards, different-sized pieces of plain paper, writing and drawing materials.

### What to do

This activity involves six children working collaboratively to produce a book. Begin by gathering the children together and read them the story *The Dark, Dark Wood* with as much expression as possible to set the scene. When you have finished, refer back to the first page and ask the children where the story starts. Write this on a piece of A5 card.

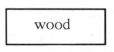

|  |
|---|
| wood |

Repeat this for each change in setting, taking the opportunity to draw the children's attention to the difference in setting on each page and noting how the space reduces from the large setting of a wood to the small context of a box.

At the end of this part of the activity you will have six cards, each depicting a scene in the story.

| wood | house | room |
|---|---|---|
| cupboard | box | ghost/mouse |

Next, work with the children to create another story beginning in the wood. Start with the card labelled 'wood' and beside it put five blank cards:

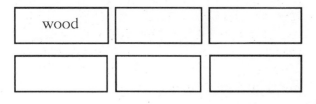

| wood |  |  |
|---|---|---|
|  |  |  |

Ask, 'What else could be in the wood?' (for example, a hill, a tree, a hole, a shed, a lake). Choose one place from the children's suggestions and ask what could be in this. Continue until all the cards have been completed. When writing the cards, encourage the children to listen to each other's ideas in order to sequence a series of settings and a story-line.

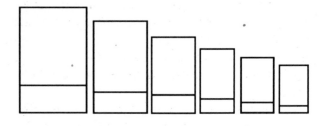

Give each of the six children one of these settings to draw, to represent the scene. It may help to provide variety in the size of paper offered to enable the children to understand that stories can take place in large and small places. Encourage those who can, to write their setting as a caption under their picture. You may have to scribe for some children.

When the children have finished, collate all of the pictures into a book with a front cover entitled 'Our book about the dark, dark wood'. This could be added to the class library or put in a special display of books.

## WATERY PLACES

### Teaching content
Physical descriptions and descriptions of sounds can help to build up a mental picture of place and settings. Different people imagine places in different ways.

### What you need
Photocopiable anthology page 93, drawing materials.

### What to do
Tell the children that you are going to read them a description. Explain that they should close their eyes and think carefully about what is being described. Ask the children to think about what kind of place this might be, what it

looks like, which colours will predominate. Read the poem 'Rain Rhymes' by Tony Mitton (from *Ashton Scholastic Collections – Early Years Poems & Rhymes* compiled by Jill Bennett, Scholastic Ltd, 1993) on photocopiable anthology page 93.

When you have finished reading the description, tell the children to open their eyes and to draw a picture of this place and how they imagined it looked. Explain that this has to be their own picture, so they should draw what they have thought about without talking to anyone else about it.

While the children are drawing, go round and talk to them about their pictures, helping them to focus on their key details.

When the drawings have been completed, pair the children and ask them to compare the pictures which they have drawn. Tell them to look for what is similar and what is different and then to ask one another why they drew the scene this way.

## ME IN DIFFERENT PLACES

### Teaching content
We have different feelings in different places. Descriptions of when, where, what and who can indicate the emotional flavour of a place.

### What you need
Chalkboard, writing and drawing materials.

### What to do
Begin by displaying a label depicting the word 'happy' to the class. With the whole class, discuss:
• When do you feel happy?
• Where do you feel happy?
• What are you doing when you are happy?
• Who is with you?
For each question, write up suggestions offered by the children on the board.

After this initial input, ask the children to draw a picture entitled 'I'm happy when I go to...' As they are drawing, discuss the pictures with individuals, encouraging them to build up a few sentences to describe this place. You may have to scribe or add words to a word bank for some children.

### Further development

This activity could be repeated at another time by changing the focus for discussion/drawing/writing to:

- In my dreams I go to...
- I would love to go to...
- I never go to...
- I hate going to...

A different place could be explored on each occasion. The procedure and key questions would be similar to the main activity in introducing, developing and concluding the session.

The children's drawings and sentences could be displayed, or collated into a series of books.

# 16

# THE DARK DEN

▣**** †††† ⑳

### Teaching content

The dark can be scary and exciting. Familiar objects can look very different and surprising.

### What you need

A safe frame that you have made, covered by blankets or a heavy dark material to blackout the den (or two low cupboards), two torches, luminous paper or material cut in a variety of shapes, for example planets, stars, faces, houses, rockets, cars, cats and so on, mirrors (make sure these are held securely), writing and drawing materials (including pens in the colours gold and silver).

### What to do

Set up the den with sufficient materials to completely cover the frame so that it is dark inside. It should have room enough for two pairs of children. (Two cupboards facing each other and a wall making up the third side makes a stable den.) Before draping the material over the frame, stick the cut-out shapes and mirrors randomly inside the den, so that when the children shine their torches they will illuminate one shape at a time.

At the start of the free-play time, explain to the children that you have set up a dark den. Tell them that two pairs of children can go in at a time and that each pair will have a torch to shine in the dark. Tell the children that if they want a surprise they should not keep the torch on all the time. Instead they should point the torch towards a section of the den and turn it on for a few seconds. If they are lucky, they might see something strange or surprising. The children can have several turns to shine the torch.

Sit near the den so that you can hear the gasps of surprise and excitement. You will also be on hand if anyone finds it 'too scary'.

At a convenient time, perhaps immediately after the den play or later during language time, talk to the children who played in the den about their play:

- What was it like in the dark den?
- What did you see/imagine when the torch went on?
- What did it feel like when the torch went off?
- Were you glad you had a friend with you?
- Would you like to go in again?

Ask the children to think about anything they found surprising when they were in the den. Tell them that you would like them to write or draw a picture of what it was like in the den to be part of a 'dark den guidebook'. Give all of the children who have participated in the den play a sheet of A4 paper with the heading 'The dark dark den'. Provide dark and shiny pens and crayons and ask the children to draw or write their guidebook page.

## 17

## AUTUMN LEAVES

### Teaching content
Place can be experienced and described, not just in visual detail, but through other senses and emotions.

### What you need
A walk in the leaves or a collection of leaves in the classroom; photocopiable anthology page 94 and photocopiable page 95, flash-card size strips of paper (enough for each member of the class), thick felt-tipped pens.

### What to do
Ideally, children should go for a walk when large piles of autumn leaves have collected in the street, the playground or the local park. (Obtain parents' permission if children are going out of the school grounds.) If this is not possible, a story about an autumn walk, and a corner set up in the classroom with piles of leaves, branches and some autumn-coloured drapery could be substituted.

What is important is that the children have the opportunity to explore the leaves in a variety of ways: the noise the leaves make when they walk through them or kick them up in the air, the smell they have, how it feels when they lift up a big handful of leaves and let them slowly flutter around their heads and back to the ground.

Pairs of children can each have a turn while the others watch and comment. You can use this time to encourage the children to think of words to describe their experiences, but try to keep this as spontaneous as possible. After everyone has had a turn to explore the leaves, ask each child to take one piece of paper and write the word which best describes his or her experience of walking in the autumn leaves. The words should be written in big letters or in a way which is like the word. There are some examples on photocopiable page 95.

At the end of the activity give each child a copy of photocopiable anthology page 94 and read the poem 'Autumn leaves' to them. Encourage them to discuss the ways in which this writing is similar to, or different from, their own work.

## 18

## MUSIC DREAMS

### Teaching content
People imagine different things; detailed description of place.

### What you need
Audio cassettes of music, cassette player, writing and drawing materials.

### What to do
To start the activity the children need to be sitting comfortably at their desks or sitting quietly on the mat, with their eyes closed. Explain that you are going to play them some music and that you want them to listen to it and imagine a place. It might be any sort of place at all; there may be people, animals, crowds or nobody at all in it.

When they are settled quietly, play the music. After a reasonable time, turn it off and ask the children to draw the place they imagined. Explain that you want them to make their drawings as detailed as possible, so they will need to concentrate on their place and draw fairly quickly, with little discussion. Then, put the children into pairs and ask them to tell their partner about the place they imagined. Finally, ask them to write about it.

Suggested music
*Carnival of the Animals*
Handel's *Water music*
Theme from *The Snowman*
*The Toys Suite*
*Lark Ascending*

## 19

## PLACE-NAMES

### Teaching content
Place-names often evoke strong images.

### What you need
Photocopiable page 96, piece of card labelled 'Greenfield Station', writing materials.
For the extension activity – a large piece of paper.

### What to do
Explain to the children that sometimes a place-name contains a clue as to what that place might look like. Give an example and show them the labelled card saying 'Greenfield Station'. Ask the children to imagine that they were going there. What do they think it would look like?

Give each child a copy of photocopiable page 96 and read the children the other five place-names. Discuss each one in turn and the picture that it might evoke.

Take one copy of photocopiable page 96 and cut out each word. Tell the children that now you are going to use the same place-names but this time you are going to mix them up. Ask them if they think the place-names will look the same. Jumble the names so that you end up with, for example:
Greenfield Castle
Shopalot Jungle
Thundermountain Station
Talltree Valley
Lionroaming Street
Spookwooky Woods

Let the children work in pairs and, using the photocopiable sheet, try to devise other names of their own. They could do this either by following through your example of cutting up, mixing and writing down new names, or by completing the blank place-name boxes given on the sheet.

Use the ideas on the photocopiable sheet and the children's suggestions to make a display of place-names, with a heading 'What do you think these places look like?'

### Further development
Ask the children to tell you the name of the street in which they live, if they know it. Extend this to exploring the names of other places they may know about. As the children offer suggestions, write these on a large piece of paper. Ask the children if they can suggest more suitable names for these familiar places.

Ask the children to complete the other sentences on the sheet in the same way, after discussing the accompanying pictures. Explain to them that the detail which they have given when writing about each picture contributes to the setting of each part of the story.

## 21

## DAYTIME/NIGHT-TIME

**\*\*\*** Ⓦ→✝ ㉚

### Teaching content
Places change and may seem very different in appearance and mood during the day and at night.

### What you need
Pieces of paper (at least A4 size) folded vertically with a thick black line down the middle, writing and drawing materials.

### What to do
Tell the children you want them to think of a place they know very well. This could be their bedroom, their classroom, or a place outside, for example their garden or the school playground.

Give each child a piece of paper with a black line down the centre. Ask the children to use coloured felt-tipped pens to draw a detailed daytime picture of this place on the left-hand side of the page. When they have finished, ask them to think about how they think this place looks at night. What changes? How would they feel in this place at night?

Next, tell them to draw a picture of the night-time place on the other side of their page. When they have finished, ask them to decide which time of day they would prefer to be in that place – daytime or night-time? What would they like about this place during their chosen time? Ask the children to write captions for their pictures, stating their preference and the reasons for it.

## 20

## ADD SOME DETAIL

**\*\*** ✝ ㉕

### Teaching content
Descriptive detail contributes to the setting.

### What you need
Photocopiable page 97, writing materials.

### What to do
Give each child a copy of photocopiable page 97. Begin by asking the children to look at the first picture which shows a picture of Goldilocks in the woods. Ask them to read the first sentence underneath the picture ('Goldilocks is in the woods'). Discuss with the children how they think Goldilocks would feel in the woods and what they think the woods would be like. Ask them to write a few words to complete the sentence 'The woods are...'

## 22

# HAPPY PLACES/SCARY PLACES

✳✳✳ ⓦ→ⅧⅢ-ⅡⅡ ③⓪

### Teaching content

Physical features can be described in ways that set the mood or atmosphere of a place. Colours, types and shapes of plants and trees, sky, weather and so on can all add to mood and atmosphere.

### What you need

Photocopiable page 98, dark paper, light paper, light and dark material, writing and drawing materials.

### What to do

Give each child a copy of photocopiable page 98. Explain that although the picture shows us the place, which comprises the mountains, fields and sky, we don't know what kind of place it is or what kind of story would happen there, because there are not enough details in the picture. Tell the children that they are going to add details to the picture to change this, but that they cannot add people or animals, only physical details. Explain that the picture could be of a happy place or a scary place, but this will depend on the colours and shapes chosen for the details. Explain that the type of sky, and the colours used for the sky, would be an important way of showing the mood of the place. The types of plants and trees and the shapes of them could also be used to indicate whether this was a happy or scary place. For children who need more support discuss this in detail.

Discuss with the children what kind of details might be added, so that when someone looked at it they would know it was a happy place. In turn, consider the sky (Is it cloudy, sunny, thundery, rainy? What are the predominant colours?), the types of plants and trees (Are they full of blossom? Bare and twisted? Do they have bright or dark colours?).

Divide the class into groups; ask one half to make their pictures scary, the other half to make their pictures happy.

While the children are drawing, go round and talk to them about their drawings. Help them to recognise how they are conveying the atmosphere by pointing out and describing key features such as black clouds and lightning, or twisted trees. This modelling of ways to describe the settings is vital. When the drawings are complete, inexperienced writers should write a short statement drawing attention to the key scary or happy feature of their drawing. For example:

• The sun shone down on the mountain.
• The mountain and fields were filled with flowers.
• The dark clouds covered the sky.

Children with more experience can write a short descriptive piece about their place, using words which describe the colours, the types of plants and how they grow, and any other features as above.

When the drawings are complete, pair the children so that they can compare a scary place with a happy place. The children should take it in turns to read their sentence or description and show their drawing. Each should note the differences from his or her own.

The finished drawings can be displayed in a mood area: mount the scary pictures and writing on dark paper, with dark material draped around them; the happy pictures on bright paper with bright material draped around them.

# I'M THINKING OF A PLACE

# 'BUT MY SCHOOL HAS...'

The teacher calls the register and collects the dinner money.

She shows the children round the classroom, and the parents too.

In the classroom there are tables chairs and drawers for the children to keep their things in. There is ...

a book corner

an interest table

a home corner

a box of dressing up clothes

and a baby rabbit in a rabbit hutch.

# THE VIEW FROM MY DOOR

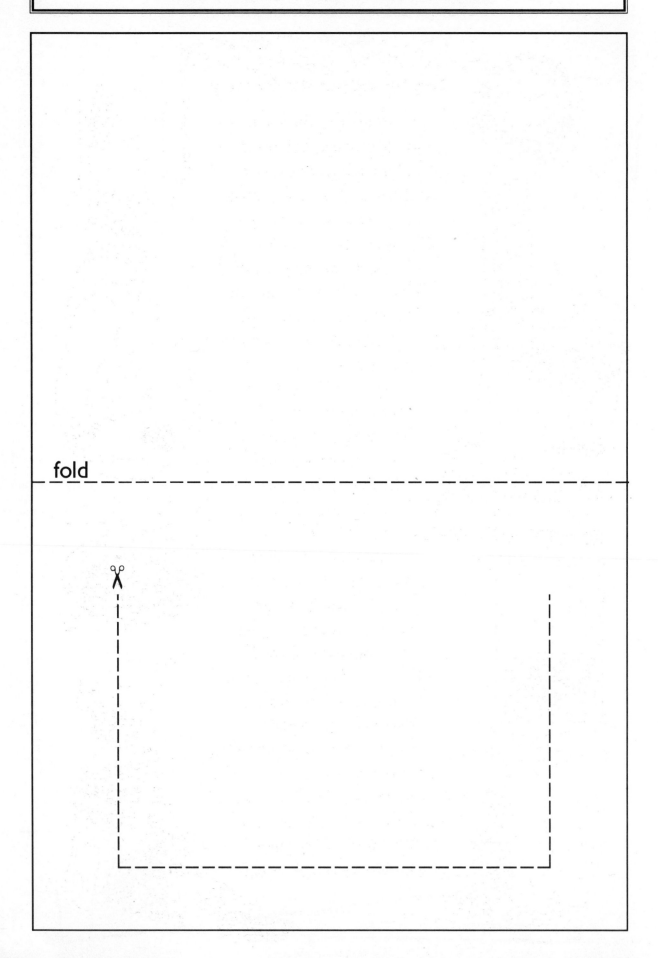

fold

# NIGHT SOUNDS/MORNING SOUNDS

## The Sounds in the Evening

The sounds in the evening
Go all through the house,
The click of the clock
And the pick of the mouse,
The footsteps of people
Upon the top floor,
The skirts of my mother
That brush by the door,
The crick in the boards,
And the creak of the chairs,
The fluttering murmurs
Outside on the stairs,
The ring of the bell,
The arrival of guests,
The laugh of my father
At one of his jests,
The clashing of dishes
As dinner goes in,
The babble of voices
That distance makes thin,
The mewings of cats
That seem just by my ear,
The hooting of owls
That can never seem near,
The queer little noises
That no one explains –
Till the moon through the slats
Of my window-blind rains,
And the world of my eyes
And my ears melts like steam
As I find in my pillow
The world of my dream.

Eleanor Farjeon

# THE WHEELS ON THE BUS

# SPECIAL BEDROOMS FOR SPECIAL PEOPLE

# MAGICAL MYSTERY TOUR

◆ Aladdin's genie says:

You can go to any two places. Where will you go?

# WATERY PLACES

## Rain Rhymes

The rain is falling on the ground.
It makes a lovely liquid sound.
A dripping splishing sploshing splashing.
In the wind, a luscious lashing.
When it drops, a peaceful plashing.
Cars are swooshing, people dashing,
Children stamping: puddle bashing.
Roofs are sheened and slates are flashing.
Slantwise lines of rain are slashing.
Sleek and shiny rain is smashing.

Tony Mitton

# AUTUMN LEAVES

**Autumn Leaves**
Down
down
down
Red
  yellow
    brown
Autumn leaves tumble down,
Autumn leaves crumble down,
Autumn leaves bumble down,
Flaking and shaking,
Tumbledown leaves.

Skittery
Flittery
Rustle by
Hustle by
Crackle and crunch
In a snappety bunch.

Run and catch
Run and snatch
Butterfly leaves
Sailboat leaves
Windstorm leaves.
Can you catch them?

Swoop,
Scoop.
Pile them up
In a stompy pile and
Jump
Jump
JUMP!

Eve Merriam

# AUTUMN LEAVES

fluttery

swishy

crunchy

scrunchy

crackly

crisp

floaty

crinkly

soggy

squelchy

swooshy

swirling

swooping

twisting

twirling

kicking

jumping

leaping

dragging

pushing

# PLACE-NAMES

| | |
|---|---|
| Greenfield | Station |
| Spookywooky | Castle |
| Shopalot | Street |
| Thundermountain | Valley |
| Talltree | Woods |
| Lionroaming | Jungle |
| | School |
| | Spaceship |

# ADD SOME DETAIL

Goldilocks is in the woods. The woods are...

Goldilocks tastes the porridge. The porridge is...

Goldilocks breaks the chair. The chair is...

Goldilocks is in the bed. The bed is...

# HAPPY PLACES/SCARY PLACES

Scholastic
**IMAGINATIVE WRITING**
Workshop

*Chapter Five*

# STORY STUCTURE

# INTRODUCTION

## What is structure?

What is it that influences a reader to pick up a book in the first place and continue to turn the pages with increasing interest in what happens next and how the story turns out in the end? The reader's involvement depends on his or her ability to understand and follow the characters and the plot, and much of this is dependent on how well the writer has structured the story.

Authors employ many structural devices to make their stories easy for the reader to follow: a title that captures attention or intrigues the reader by giving a hint about the story; the use of an opening that draws the reader in, perhaps because it is something familiar and promises a return to a remembered pleasure, or because it is unexpected or puzzling; the development of the plot in sequence and the use of viewpoint, cliff-hangers and turning points to hold the reader's attention or change the pace of events. All these serve to keep the reader involved and make him or her want to turn the page until the end, where the conclusion draws together the loose ends of the story and resolves the problems to create a complete and emotionally satisfying story.

## What do young children know about story structure?

From their experience of stories, very young children build up an implicit understanding of story structure. Two- and three-year olds protest loudly if the reader attempts to miss out or paraphrase part of a story. For them, stories have one correct sequence of events and can be told only in one way: that which the author first determines. This forms part of their enjoyment, allowing them the satisfaction of predicting the story with complete certainty, as well as the entertainment of reliving the story events with each retelling.

Once young children have become familiar with a story, they use their knowledge of story structure to help them retell the story events. In retelling, however, children often adapt and change the story, focusing on those parts they most enjoyed and thus altering its content and structure. Structure, therefore, provides the scaffolding whereby children go beyond the

story they have heard to create a version which becomes their own. This process of retelling and remaking stories through play or conversation is important because it teaches children that stories need not be set in stone. When young children react by being interested, surprised or excited by changed versions, they have understood this important aspect of storytelling, and their knowledge of structure has played a key role in this development.

## Structure in stories for young children

Stories for young children often make particular use of distinct, unambiguous structural features, which give clear signals and work together to capture and maintain the children's interest. Straightforward titles help young story-seekers to tune in to what the story will be about. Repetitive patterns and phrases within the story help them to become accustomed to the sequence quickly, so that they know what to expect. Endings are often stylised but always emotionally satisfying, leaving the reader with a feeling of satisfaction that ensures a desire to repeat the experience.

For example, Rod Campbell in *Dear Zoo* tells a story of a child writing to the zoo for a pet. This story enthrals young children, yet each page has almost identical text:

> I wrote to the zoo to send me a pet
> They sent me an...
> (elephant).
> He was too big so I sent him back.
> So they sent me a...
> (frog).
> He was too jumpy so I sent him back...

Children make sense of *Dear Zoo* because of the repetition in ideas and form. However, the excitement and suspense of the story is heightened by the layout of the book – the text is broken up so that the first page of each episode ends with an incomplete sentence 'So they sent me a...' To complete the sentence, the child must look at the next page and lift a flap to see the illustration. This pause at a crucial point in the story-line heightens the suspense and involvement of young readers, drawing them into the story by giving them time to predict what could happen next and giving them some physical control of the reading process through lifting the flap and uncovering the unsuitable animal beneath. Other features also encourage prediction – the shape, size and type of containers and the use of large block capitals and bold lettering for words like 'DANGER' (for the lion) and 'VERY HEAVY' (for the elephant). The final page provides an ending in keeping with the simple repetition of the other pages, but is emotionally satisfying to the reader:

> So they thought very hard and sent me a...
> (puppy).
> He was perfect! So I kept him.

The use of exclamations and exaggerated expressions to draw children's attention to essential characters or emphasise the repetitive nature of the story is very common in children's books and stories. In *The Three Billy Goats Gruff*, the troll says 'Who's that trip trapping over MY bridge?' This gives the children an opportunity to participate in the story, but also signals the repetitive structure, helping them to recognise that this situation has occurred before and is now repeated with a slight variation in the characters involved.

Television, films (especially cartoons) and comics are often key story experiences for children, and they highlight the essence of the story in similar ways. They make use of exaggerated graphical or textual facilities to make the message clear and accentuate key points.

Writers of stories for young children thus use simplified and readily comprehended structures and structural devices but, as in the *Dear Zoo* example, bring them together in sophisticated ways.

### Teaching about structure

Young children make unconscious structural decisions about their writing. However, teachers need to ensure that children have a range of experiences that target different aspects of structure by encouraging children to think about:

- The title. What should it do?
- What makes a good beginning?
- Whose story is this? Who is telling it?
- What are the key events in the story and how are they best sequenced for the reader?
- How can the story be segmented to sustain interest, create suspense or pace?
- What makes a good ending?

When teachers and children share stories in the classroom, the structural features can often be highlighted naturally and in context simply by reading the story well, for example by taking time to turn a crucial page, thus underlining a device for creating suspense. Similarly,

discussion with the children before and after the story can raise important issues about the role and effect of titles, beginnings and endings. 'This looks like an interesting title! I wonder what the story will be about?
I like the parts in the story where the author...
How did you know that was going to happen?
Did you like the ending/beginning?
Was that what you wanted to happen to...?'

When children create stories, they rehearse structural decisions by playing, relating or drawing pictures of their stories. This helps them identify and sequence the key events, clarify the story-line and determine the viewpoint from which the story will be told. By recognising the value of such activities in supporting the young child's decision making, the teacher enables structural decisions to become incorporated into the way that the child actually wants to tell the story, rather than being imposed in a rigid and formal way through, for example, a story planning sheet.

In this way, children are reminded that they are writing their story for someone to read and enjoy. Keeping this in mind is often the best way to raise the structural decisions which have to be made.

## CONTENTS AND ORGANISATION

The activities in this chapter focus on four different aspects of structure: sequencing the plot; titles, layout and divisions; beginnings and endings; and points of view. Each of these is explained below.

### Sequencing the plot

Some stories for young children work because they draw on children's knowledge from elsewhere to provide a predictable sequence for the plot: the days of the week, as in *The Very Hungry Caterpillar* by Eric Carle; the number sequence in *Mr Magnolia* by Quentin Blake or *The Shopping Basket* by John Burningham; the hours of the day, as in Eric Carle's *The Bad-Tempered Ladybird*; the rooms of a building, as in *A Scary Story* by Peter Bailey or in a *A Dark, Dark Tale* by Ruth Brown; or the sequence of a journey, as in the *Berenstain Bears Series* of spooky stories by Jan Berenstain or the stories about *Mr Gumpy* by John Burningham.

Other stories derive their structure in ways

that are perhaps more familiar to the adult reader; they begin with the characters and setting and then a problem occurs. The story is driven by the need to resolve this problem. Children will be familiar with a range of possible problems: the problematic character trait, as in *The Trouble with Mum* by Babette Cole, or *Alex's Bed* by Mary Dickinson; the lost item, as in *Dogger* by Shirley Hughes; the accident or unexpected event, as in *Funnybones* by Janet Ahlberg; the chance meeting, as in *Red Riding Hood*; or a 'naughty' character, as in *This is the Bear and the Picnic Lunch* by Sarah Hayes. This is not an exhaustive list. Both children and teachers will be able to find many more books with different types of problems occurring, all of which serve to put the story events into motion and propel the story forward.

## How can children be helped to sequence the plot?

In play, children identify the essence of a story by adopting exaggerated mannerisms and by playing out the climax, the most exciting point, over and over again. When children write their stories, this is the part that they most want to describe. Young writers often want to write down the most exciting parts without explaining to the reader how the story started, where it took place, who was involved and what led up to the key event. The activities in this section, therefore, have been designed to help children to recognise that:

• stories don't start at the most exciting part. Crafting a story involves preparing the readers by setting the scene, introducing the characters and stating the 'problem' before leading up to the key event. This can be done through activities in which children sequence stories, complete the 'missing parts' of stories or identify the beginning, middle and end;

• they can use a variety of practical strategies to help them generate and sequence a story: imaginative play using the dressing-up box; 'small worlds' play using toys as characters to act out the story; using puppets; drawing; or simply talking with others, can all help children to determine the sequence and focus of their stories.

Through engaging in story-making activities which use these different strategies, children will begin to understand the difference between them and the potential and the limitations of each.

Stories can be driven by different types of problem or structures. The problems may be internal – to do with the inherent nature of the characters or place – or they may be external – something happens or someone arrives. Structure-driven stories may be derived from any sequence the child knows well: days of the week, months, hours, numbers and so on. The important thing is that children need experience of reading, playing and writing a range of different types of story so that they become familiar with the range of structures possible.

## Titles, layout and divisions

Children often know that the title attracts the reader to the story and that, along with the cover illustration, it may reveal information about the characters, the events, the mood or the type of story. They need to be taught that choosing a title is often best left to the end of the writing process and that the final title may be different from their working title. Once children know what they have written, they will be better able to identify and capture the essence of the story.

Children, and many adults, are often unaware of the subtle influence that the divisions and layout of a story can exert on a reader. How the story is split into sections, or laid out on the pages, can be a key device in making the reader want to read on or read in a particular way. In *Dear Zoo*, a pause in the text does this. In the book *A Scary Story*, the layout and divisions help to create both the slowly growing apprehension and the panic as the cats run away at the end. The large pictures and regular, predictable text create a long, slow build-up as the cats become increasingly frightened and hesitant. This is in strong contrast to their helter-skelter retreat, when the text is short or non-existent and the pictures are closer together, increasing the pace of the story.

The activities in this section provide writing and reading experiences which encourage children to notice, think about and discuss the effect of layout on the reader.

## Beginnings and endings

Children need to know that story beginnings have to hook the reader and that this can be done by setting the scene, introducing the key characters, by plunging into a key event or problem, or by using stylistic devices such as 'Once upon a time...' Similarly, they need to know that endings are important to the reader's enjoyment. Young children enjoy endings that are unambiguous and emotionally satisfying ones which resolve the problems and tie up all the loose ends. This section contains activities which draw their attention to these aspects.

## Points of view

Children need to learn that stories can be told from different points of view. For example, although both *Dear Zoo* and *The House Cat* tell stories about children acquiring a pet, the use of the cat's point of view in the latter provides an intriguing and different angle on the story and determines how it is told. Young children may well find it difficult to tell a story from someone else's point of view, or through the eyes of the key character, in a way which provides consistency and detail. Yet through the activities in this section, children can be encouraged to recognise these issues in their reading and to explore them through play, drama and stories.

## Bibliography – children's books

*Dear Zoo*, Rod Campbell (1985) Picture Puffin
*The Very Hungry Caterpillar*, Eric Carle (1995) Puffin
*Mr Magnolia*, Quentin Blake (1981) Fontana
*The Shopping Basket*, John Burningham (1983) Fontana
*The Bad-Tempered Ladybird*, Eric Carle (1994) Puffin
*A Dark, Dark Tale*, Ruth Brown (1992) Red Fox
*The Trouble with Mum*, Babette Cole (1985) Collins
*Alex's Bed*, Mary Dickinson (1981) Hippo Books
*Dogger*, Shirley Hughes (1993) Red Fox
*Funnybones*, Janet Ahlberg (1980) Heinemann
*This is the Bear and the Picnic Lunch*, Sarah Hayes (1988) Walker Books

| Activity | Teaching content | Star rating | Group size | Photo-copiable |
|---|---|---|---|---|
| 1 Sequencing the story-line | Story sequence; stories don't start at the most exciting part | */** | 1/2 | ✓✓✓✓ |
| 2 If I met... | Contrasting characters can drive a story | * | Ⓦ⇨2⇨4 | ✓ |
| 3 Untidy Alex 1 | The main character can drive a story | * | 4 | A |
| 4 Untidy Alex 2 | Stories need characters, a problem, development and solution | **/*** | 4⇨2 | ✓ |
| 5 What happened next? | Stories from character and action combinations | ** | 4⇨2 | ✓✓ |
| 6 Once upon a time | Stories from character and setting combinations | */** | Ⓦ⇨1/2 | ✓ |
| 7 What does the cover tell us? | The book cover can indicate story content | * | 4 | ✓A |
| 8 What's at the bottom of the garden? | Titles and illustrations support story content | */** | 4⇨2 | ✓ |
| 9 Find a title | Title and layout support the story | */*** | 4⇨2 | ✓✓ |
| 10 Traditional titles, traditional tales? | Choosing the best title is a matter of opinion | *** | Ⓦ⇨2 | |
| 11 What story will this be? | Title, opening lines and the book cover can all indicate the type of story | *** | Ⓦ | |
| 12 The scariest book | The beginning of a story helps to create the appropriate mood | */*** | Ⓦ⇨1 | A |
| 13 What *did* happen? | Ingredients for a good ending | ** | 4⇨2 | ✓ |
| 14 Conversational endings | A conversation can 'round off' and conclude the story | **/*** | Ⓦ⇨2 | ✓ |
| 15 Fairy-tale endings | Stories can be told in different ways | *** | Ⓦ | ✓ |
| 16 Making a story collection | Stories can be told from different viewpoints | */*** | Ⓦ | |
| 17 Who is telling the story? | Stories can be told from different viewpoints | */*** | 4⇨1 | ✓✓✓ |
| 18 Our dad/those children | Actions can be described from different viewpoints | **/*** | 2 | ✓ |

A = photocopiable anthology page
Ⓦ = whole group

Give the children the appropriate photocopiable sheet. Establish that the pictures relate to the events in the book but that they are all in the wrong order. Allow the children to work individually or in pairs, and explain that they must cut out the pictures and put them into the correct sequence on the concertina book pages.

If appropriate, ask the children to sequence the sentences by cutting them out and pasting each section of text below the correct picture.

This activity can be repeated using each of the books listed in 'What you need' and the photocopiable pages providing accompanying sequence sheets.

## 1

## SEQUENCING THE STORY-LINE

### Teaching content

Stories have a beginning, middle and end. They don't start at the most exciting or the best part.

### What you need

The story books *Get Lost, Laura!*, *The House Cat*, *Mr Pam Pam and the Hullabazoo*, *Blooming Cats*, a photocopiable sheet chosen from pages 116–119, scissors, glue, blank concertina books, writing materials.

### What to do

Choose one book for this activity from those listed above. Read the book to the children, giving them plenty of opportunity to discuss the pictures and enjoy the story. Once the story has been read and discussed, briefly revise the main events by returning to the first page and summarising what happens in each of the main pictures.

## 2

## IF I MET...

### Teaching content

The reaction of one character to another can propel the story forward.

### What you need

Photocopiable page 120, chalkboard/A3 paper.

### What to do

The children should be familiar with a range of traditional stories and the wicked characters depicted in them. Give each pair a copy of photocopiable page 120 and tell them to decide what they would do if they met each of these characters. The first incomplete sentence reads 'If I met the big bad wolf I would...' The children then write or draw what they would do. Model how to do this by taking the first character, the big, bad wolf, and brainstorming a range of suggestions. List these on the board or write them on a sheet of A3 paper to make a poster. There are some examples in the first column below.

| | |
|---|---|
| gobble him up | 'I'm not afraid of you!' |
| run away | 'I'm going to eat YOU up!' |
| punch his nose | 'I don't like you.' |
| pull his tail | 'You can't catch me!' |
| hide | 'What a lovely wolf you are!' |
| cry | 'Look out, I'm behind you!' |
| kiss him | A loud scream |

Tell the children to think of what they would do if they met each of the other characters and to write or draw this in the space provided on the photocopiable sheet. Let the children take it in turns in their pairs to make suggestions and write or draw.

Then they should think of what they would say and write this down. When the children have finished, put them into groups of four and let them read their suggestions to one another.

### Further development

Try similar activities with good, funny or brave characters from well-known stories.

### Teaching content

Stories can be driven by inherent qualities in a character which others react to.

### What you need

Photocopiable anthology page 121 and photocopiable page 56, display board, glue, writing materials, four caption cards: (1) Mum

says (2) Alex's best friend says (3) Captain Clean says (4) Milly Messy says.

### What to do

Make an A3-sized copy of photocopiable anthology page 121. This is an illustration from the book *Alex's Bed* by Mary Dickinson (Hippo Books, 1981) which shows Alex in his untidy room. Pin the picture on a display board where children can see it. You can add speech bubbles (made from copies of photocopiable page 56) and captions around the picture during the activity. Discuss with the children the mess in Alex's room: 'Look at Alex's room! What do you think of it?'

Now ask the children what they think his mum would say when she comes into the room. After hearing several suggestions, pin the caption card 'Mum says' and a blank speech bubble (cut out from a copy of photocopiable page 56, enlarged if necessary) on the display board near the picture and tell the children that you are going to write in it what the author thought Mum would say.

> Mum says, 'Why won't you ever put anything away?'

Ask the children: 'Is this what you thought Mum would say? Is it nearly the same or quite different? What kind of voice would Mum have?'

Then tell the children to imagine that three other people came into Alex's room that day and each one said something different. Now the children have to be the authors and decide what each person would say and how they would say it. Pin up the caption 'Alex's best friend says'. Talk to the children about Alex's best friend. 'Who do you think Alex's best friend is? What will the best friend think of Alex's room? Will the friend like it or not? What will they want to do in the untidy room? What will the best friend say?'

Take a few suggestions and then choose one which seems appropriate, funny or surprising. Write this on another speech bubble. Ask the children, 'How does the best friend say it? Will it be like Mum's voice or different?'

Now pin up the caption for Captain Clean and explain that it is his job to keep the world tidy. Ask the children, 'What do you think he would say about Alex's room? How would he speak?' Again, agree on what he would say and add this to a speech bubble.

Do the same for Milly Messy, the girl who loves a mess. At the end, look back at the different things people said and the different ways they spoke.

*Note:* Ideally, this activity should precede the next one, although they are not interdependent.

### Further development
Similar activities might be tried with other characters, for example Hannah in *Hannah's Temper* by Celia Berridge (André Deutsch, 1992).

### Teaching content
Story structures often have the following key parts: the characters, the 'problem', the development, the solution and the conclusion.

### What you need
A copy of *Alex's Bed* by Mary Dickinson (Hippo Books, 1981), completed display board from the previous activity 'Untidy Alex 1' (these first two items are preferable, but not essential), three large oblong pieces of card, photocopiable page 122, writing materials.

### What to do
Read or tell the children the story of *Alex's Bed*. (Although having a copy of *Alex's Bed* is not essential, it would enhance the activity if the story were read to the children. The synopsis in the box can be used if the book is unavailable.)

Remind the children about Untidy Alex and tell them the whole story of *Alex's Bed* – what happened after Mum said 'Why won't you ever put anything

> Alex's bedroom is a mess – just like a dump, his mum says. The only bit of space they can find in the whole room is up by the ceiling.
> 'I know,' says Mum, 'Why not put your bed up in the space? Then there will be lots of space where the bed is now!'
> So, off they go to the wood shop to buy what they need to make long, long legs for the bed. A bed on stilts! And then, of course, they need to make a ladder so Alex can reach the bed. And a safety rail so that he doesn't fall out. And a hanging bedside table to put his things on!
> And when all of this is done, Alex's untidy room is... still untidy! Because Alex is... well, Alex!

away?' Tell the children that you want them to pick out the three main parts of the story. Discuss with the children how the story starts and what seems to be the problem. When the children have identified the problem write it on the first piece of card: 'The problem: there is no room – the only space is near the ceiling.'

Now talk to the children about what Alex and his mum decide to do to solve the problem. This may take quite a lot of discussion as there was a lot of detail about the solution, but you should finally agree with the children and write on the second piece of card: 'The solution: to build a high bed.'

Now talk to the children about how the story ended. Did the solution solve all the problems? Help the children to identify how the story ended. Write on the final piece of card: 'The conclusion: Alex was still untidy.'

Now tell the children that they are going to work in pairs. Give each pair of children a copy of photocopiable page 122. Tell each pair to choose one of the other characters from the poster created in the previous activity (or another character of their own). They should draw a picture of the character and write down what he or she said to Alex in the speech bubble at the top of the page. Next to the first picture of Alex's untidy room are the words 'There is no room' – the 'problem'. At the bottom of the page the conclusion is written: 'Alex is still untidy!' But each pair must decide how to fill the empty middle box with a solution. If the children have not done this before you may want to work with the whole group and model with them several likely suggestions for solutions for each character. For example, Milly Messy: remind the children that Milly was the messiest girl in the world and talk about what her reactions to Alex's room were. Now list some suggestions for Milly Messy's solution:
'Let's throw it all out of the window.
Let's put a notice on the door, "Only untidy people allowed inside this room".'

Children can now draw or write a solution in the empty box to complete the skeleton of the story structure.

# WHAT HAPPENED NEXT?

### Teaching content

Stories may have a beginning, middle and end. Different combinations of characters and action can create different stories, with different endings.

### What you need

Photocopiable pages 123 and 124, writing materials.

### What to do

Gather the group together round a table and show them the character cards on photocopiable page 123. Discuss each of the characters in turn and what they are doing. Select one as an exemplar to work through with the group. Cut out the picture and stick it on to the first frame on the storyboard on photocopiable page 124. Using the accompanying caption beneath, choose a name for the character to begin the story and write this in the space provided, '... was walking along the street quite happily when...'

Next show the children the story actions on photocopiable page 123. Read through them with the children and ask them to select one for the next part of the story. When they have chosen one, cut this out and paste it in the second box on the storyboard. Draw a picture in the frame above showing the action that has been described.

Now draw the children's attention to the sequencing/linking word 'and'. Discuss with them possible solutions to bring their story to an end. Write this in the third box to complete the story and draw a final picture in the box above. Explain to the children that if the characters and/or the action had been different the story would also have been different. Show them how a variety of stories could be made up using the cards.

Now, with the children working in pairs, give out both photocopiable sheets. Tell the children that you want them to make up another story in just the same way. You may need to scribe or provide words for some children – most of the input will be needed in predicting the end of the story and discussing their reasons for ending it in this way. Use this opportunity to talk about the ending – is it happy, sad, funny or exciting?

Finally, when each pair has finished, allow time for them to read their stories to the other

children in the group. As the nature of this activity lends itself to a variety of stories being created, it is a useful activity to leave in a writing area for free choice in story building.

### Further development
Read the children  *Each Peach Pear Plum* (Picture Puffin, 1989) and *The Jolly Postman or Other People's Letters* (Heinemann, 1995) both by Janet and Allan Ahlberg.

### ONCE UPON A TIME

### Teaching content
Stories can arise from characters and places. Changing the character/place combination can change the story.

### What you need
Photocopiable page 125, chalkboard, writing materials.

### What to do
Show the children the two columns on photocopiable page 125 and read them through with the group or class. Ensure the children understand that the text on the left-hand side of the page tells you about characters and the text on the right-hand side tells you about places.

Begin by asking the children to suggest suitable places for those characters with whom they are familiar. Then, point out that other character/place matchings are also possible, although they would not lead to the fairy stories they know so well. For example, 'A girl called Goldilocks who... lived under a bridge.'

Ask the children whether this could lead to another story. Why might Goldilocks be living under the bridge? What would her home look like (nothing like a troll's home, for sure!)? Who would, or could, she meet in this story and what would happen?

Explore the story possibilities of different pairings on the photocopiable sheet. Then point out that the final two place/action spaces are blank. Can the children suggest places that might suit the fat frog or the wicked witch, but not some of the earlier characters? Record their suggestions on the board.

When you feel that children have a sufficient idea of the activity, ask them to work individually or in pairs. Tell the children to choose, from the ideas on photocopiable page 125 or the board, any character/place pairing they like and to write the story, either together or individually, as appropriate. Once the story has been written, they should devise a suitable title.

### WHAT DOES THE COVER TELL US?

### Teaching content
The front cover of a book can provide a lot of discussion and prediction about the content of the book.

### What you need
Photocopiable anthology page 126 and photocopiable page 127, wrapping paper, writing and drawing materials (including A4 paper).

### What to do
Gather the group together, either round a table or in the library area. Show the children the cover of the book 'Paul's Present' on

photocopiable anthology page 126. Involve the children in looking closely at the cover, the title and the detail of the illustrations in order to predict what the content may be about and to draw on the children's own experiences of presents. The following questions may be of use in framing a discussion session:

• What and who do you think this book might be about?
• What makes you think that? On the front cover, what gives you a clue?
• What kinds of presents do you think there may be in the book?
• Why do you think Paul may be getting a present?
• What kind of person is Paul? How do you know?

Individually, ask each child to think of, then tell you about, a present that they would like to draw themselves holding. Ask each child to describe the present and encourage the other children within the group to ask questions about it also. Then give each child a sheet of A4 paper and tell the children that you would like them to design a cover for their own book about their present. Talk about starting with the main picture, just like in 'Paul's Present', then filling in a surrounding border with a choice of smaller drawings to suit their story about a present.

When the drawings have been completed, the children should select a piece of wrapping paper and cut it to an appropriate size to cover the picture of their present, thereby forming a 'flap' to be lifted up. Again, this will provide a good opportunity for the children to work together, predicting what might be hidden under the wrapping paper. It may even lead to another book!

As the children are drawing, use this opportunity to talk with each child individually about:
• the present they received;
• when they got it;
• what they did with it.

### Further development

The discussion about the children's presents in the final part of the activity would be useful as a stimulus for a 'further development' activity in which the children use a copy of photocopiable page 127 to write a three-part story. Ask the children to answer each of the questions, which provide a framework for their story. This writing part of the activity could be carried out on another occasion, within the next few days.

# WHAT'S AT THE BOTTOM OF THE GARDEN?

### Teaching content
The title needs to match the illustrations and reflect the story.

### What you need
Photocopiable page 128, cut and stick labels, writing materials.

### What to do
Begin by reading the children the extract from *The Selfish Giant* by Oscar Wilde below.

> It was a large lovely garden, with soft green grass. Here and there over the grass stood beautiful flowers like stars, and there were twelve peach-trees that in the spring-time broke out into delicate blossoms of pink and pearl, and in the autumn bore rich fruit. The birds sat on the trees and sang so sweetly that the children used to stop their games in order to listen to them.

Discuss with the children the type of garden and the mood the mind-picture of it evokes. What kind of garden is this? What does it make you feel like? Do you think it is a happy garden, a scary garden, a magical garden or a funny garden? What is it about the description that makes you think this? What kind of story do you think might happen in a garden like this? Reread the passage to the children several times if necessary.

Ask the children what might make a good title for a story about a garden like this. List a number of suggestions, for example 'In the magic garden', 'The garden of happiness', 'The beautiful garden'.

Ask the children to work in pairs and to choose one of the garden pictures on photocopiable page 128. Tell the children to think carefully about the kind of story that might happen in a garden like the one they have chosen and then to think of a good title for a story about the garden.

## FIND A TITLE

### Teaching content

The front cover and title tell you about the book. The title may be short or long. This activity will also encourage children to think through the process of story building.

### What you need

Photocopiable pages 129 and 130, writing materials.

### What to do

Explain to the children that for this activity they are going to design a front cover for a story book. Using the exemplar on photocopiable page 129, talk through the process with the children. Start by talking about the picture:
• What do you think this story could be about?
• Where might the burglar be?
• What could be in the safe?
• Why is the burglar trying to break into the safe?

• What will the burglar do with what is in the safe?
• Do you think the burglar is about to open or close the safe? Why?
• Is there anything else you might want to add to this picture – a bag of jewels; a window for a quick escape; a torch shining on to the burglar; a hand (with a blue uniform visible at the wrist) touching the burglar's shoulder?

Record their suggestions on the sheet in the space below the picture and ask the children to suggest a title for the picture. Discuss with the children how some titles may be very short – one word – and some may be a sentence. For example 'Burglar' or 'Caught!' could become 'Burglar Bill and the stolen treasure'. Ask them to select from their suggestions the one which they like best and record it on a copy of photocopiable page 129.

Draw the children's attention to the word 'burglar', which has been used as a possible title, and the different styles in which the word has been written. It may be useful to draw children's attention to other titles of books and the different typefaces that are used, and to leave these on the table to stimulate ideas.

Now, ask the children to work in pairs and select one picture from a copy of photocopiable page 130. Explain the process, using photocopiable page 129 as a model for:
• jotting down their ideas about their picture;
• deciding upon a title for their picture and recording their idea in the box;
• then trying out different ways to write this.

They should then cut out their chosen picture from photocopiable page 130 and stick it on to a plain sheet of A4 paper, using a copy of photocopiable page 129 as a model for positioning. Tell them to write their title in their chosen typeface/format on the page and perhaps add a colourful border to complete their cover.

Finally, provide an opportunity for the pairs to show their 'covers' to the others in the group and allow them to guess what the other stories may be about.

This activity stands on its own, but may be extended to the story being developed by the children over a period of time.

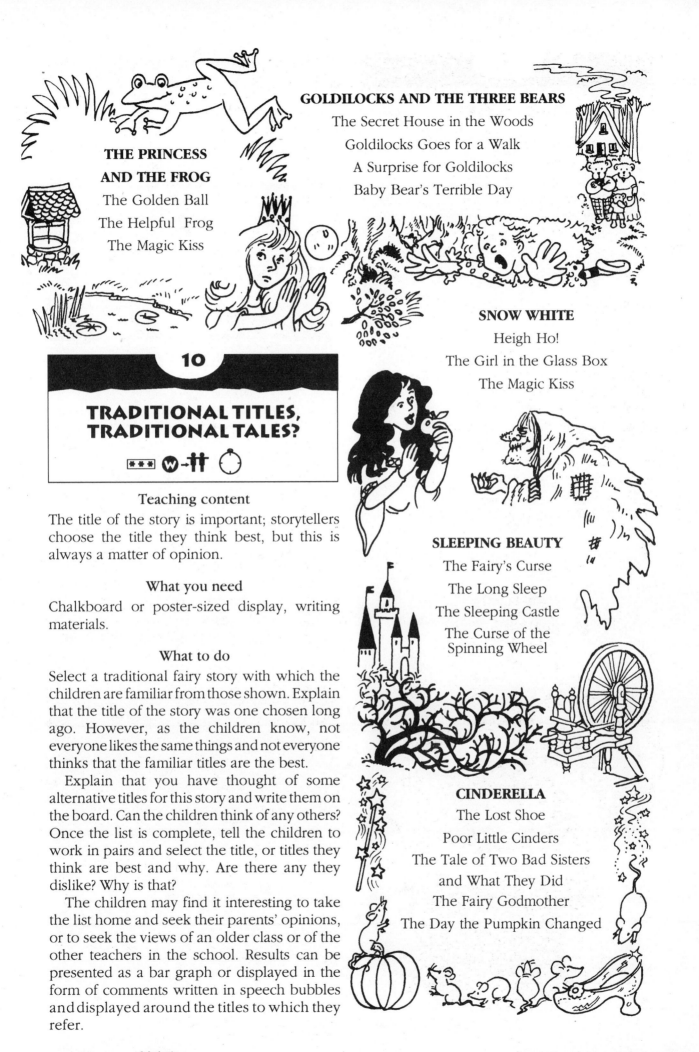

**THE PRINCESS AND THE FROG**

The Golden Ball
The Helpful Frog
The Magic Kiss

**GOLDILOCKS AND THE THREE BEARS**

The Secret House in the Woods
Goldilocks Goes for a Walk
A Surprise for Goldilocks
Baby Bear's Terrible Day

**SNOW WHITE**

Heigh Ho!
The Girl in the Glass Box
The Magic Kiss

**SLEEPING BEAUTY**

The Fairy's Curse
The Long Sleep
The Sleeping Castle
The Curse of the Spinning Wheel

**CINDERELLA**

The Lost Shoe
Poor Little Cinders
The Tale of Two Bad Sisters
and What They Did
The Fairy Godmother
The Day the Pumpkin Changed

## 10

# TRADITIONAL TITLES, TRADITIONAL TALES?

### Teaching content

The title of the story is important; storytellers choose the title they think best, but this is always a matter of opinion.

### What you need

Chalkboard or poster-sized display, writing materials.

### What to do

Select a traditional fairy story with which the children are familiar from those shown. Explain that the title of the story was one chosen long ago. However, as the children know, not everyone likes the same things and not everyone thinks that the familiar titles are the best.

Explain that you have thought of some alternative titles for this story and write them on the board. Can the children think of any others? Once the list is complete, tell the children to work in pairs and select the title, or titles they think are best and why. Are there any they dislike? Why is that?

The children may find it interesting to take the list home and seek their parents' opinions, or to seek the views of an older class or of the other teachers in the school. Results can be presented as a bar graph or displayed in the form of comments written in speech bubbles and displayed around the titles to which they refer.

## WHAT STORY WILL THIS BE?

### Teaching content
The cover, title and opening sentences of a book can all indicate what a story will be like.

### What you need
Children's story books (including ones which have front covers that do not obviously illustrate the content conveyed by the text at the beginning of the story), for example *A Dark, Dark Tale* (Red Fox, 1992) and *The Big Sneeze* (Beaver, 1986), both by Ruth Brown, and *The Enchanted Wood* (Little, Brown, 1992) by Ruth Sanderson.

### What to do
Select one or two children's story books. Show the children the titles and the front covers and read the first few sentences of the story. Then stop and ask them what sort of a story they think it will be. Is it one they will like? Why? How do they know? Note which children find it easy to make quick and reliable judgements and which are more hesitant or less reliable.

Now tell the children that you are going to give them a more difficult task. Tell them that you are going to read them the title and the first sentence of a book, but *not* show them the front cover. They must listen carefully and, as before, try to decide the sort of story this will be

and whether they will like it. Then read the title and the opening paragraph from your chosen book to the children. Some children will find this task much more difficult, but it is important that they are encouraged to think about how the title and opening paragraph can indicate the story content, without relying solely on the illustrations. Finally, show the children the front cover of the book. Given this additional information, do the children wish to change or add to their predictions about the type of story and its content? Why?

## THE SCARIEST BOOK

### Teaching content
The beginning of a story helps the reader to recognise what kind of story it will be and helps to create an appropriate mood and expectations.

### What you need
Photocopiable anthology page 131, writing and drawing materials.

### What to do
Give each child a copy of photocopiable anthology page 131. Read the first piece of text to the children. Talk to them about what they think the story will be about. Ask them what makes them think this. Establish with the children that this might be a scary or frightening story.

Do the same for the second story beginning and establish that these are both scary stories. Ask the children how the author has made us think this. What words or phrases has the author used? Tell the children to write down which words and phrases they think are 'scary'.

Then ask the children to draw a picture to match the text from one of the scary stories on the photocopiable sheet. To conclude the activity, ask the children to choose which story they think is the scariest. The pictures of their stories could be cut out, mounted and displayed in the story corner with a large caption of the story beginning.

### Further development
Similar activities could be used for funny, sad, magical or adventure stories.

# WHAT *DID* HAPPEN?

**\*\* ‖‖‖·‖‖ (30)**

### Teaching content

What makes a good ending to a story?

### What you need

The story *Goldilocks and the Three Bears*, photocopiable page 132, glue, scissors, writing materials.

### What to do

Begin by reading the story of *Goldilocks and the Three Bears* to the group. Probably, the ending will show Goldilocks running away, but you may have different versions of the story with alternative endings. These would be particularly useful, to show the children that there can be more than one way to end a story. Sometimes stories don't always end the way we would like them to and we think 'if only...' or 'I wish that...' had happened. This type of discussion would be useful to focus on endings and to look at what else might have happened when Goldilocks woke up.

Give each child a copy of photocopiable page 132 and read the text in the first box to the children. Ask them to predict what she could have said/shouted/screamed/whispered.

Role-play may also be useful within the group at this point. Allocate the roles of Goldilocks and the three bears or ask for volunteers. Through this medium, ask different 'Goldilocks' children what *they* would say and do as a result of seeing the bears leaning over them and staring at them.

Return to the photocopiable sheet and, working in pairs, let the children decide which verb to use from the selection at the foot of the page (said, shouted, screamed, whispered). Ask the children to write the verb they have chosen in the box provided, or to write a different word if they have decided upon an alternative verb. Then ask the children to fill in what Goldilocks said in the speech bubble in the second box.

Finally, ask the children to predict and decide upon a new ending to their version of the story. They should write this in the third box on the photocopiable sheet and draw a picture below the text.

To conclude the session, ask each pair to

read their 'endings' to the other children in the group. The sheets could be collated on a frieze or in a class book entitled 'What *did* happen to Goldilocks?'

# 14

# CONVERSATIONAL ENDINGS

**\*\*\*\*\* ⓦ·‖‖ ○**

### Teaching content

Stories can end in different ways. They can end with a conversation.

### What you need

Photocopiable page 133, chalkboard, writing materials.

### What to do

Ensure that the children are familiar with the story of *The Three Little Pigs*. Explain that this story sometimes ends with all the pigs safely at the home of the little pig who built his house out of bricks. The children will have heard other versions, however, and should be encouraged to relate these. As they do so, record them on the board.

Ask the children to choose one ending to write about (or allocate an ending, if this is more appropriate). Explain that the writer could end the story with a conversation. The three little pigs could each say something about the story and what has happened to them. Write suggestions on the board. Ask the children to choose or invent their own conversation and then, working in pairs, write their words in the speech bubbles on a copy of photocopiable page 133.

Explain that any conversation could be used to form a new ending for a story.

### Teaching content
The same story can be told in different ways; writers make choices about how they tell a story.

### What you need
The story of *Cinderella* (several versions of this fairy tale), photocopiable page 134, A3 paper. For the extension activities – versions of another popular tale.

### What to do
Read the children the story of *Cinderella*, but stop just before you get to the end. Show the children the endings on a copy of photocopiable page 134 (enlarge it to A3 size if necessary) which illustrate three different ways of ending the story:
• with the traditional 'happy ever after' ending;
• with a conversation between two characters;
• with a description of a scene.

Explain that the story could end in any one of these ways. Which do the children prefer and why? Suggest the children bring in other examples of this popular fairy-tale and make a display of all the different versions they find. Take opportunities to read the various versions to the children and discuss the similarities and differences, which they like most and why.

### Further development 1
This idea can be applied to other popular fairy tales (*Little Red Riding Hood, The Billy Goats Gruff, Goldilocks*) by getting the children to

write endings, collect different versions to make a display and then discussing which they like best.

### Further development 2
Apply this same activity to the beginnings of stories.

### Teaching content
The same story can be told from different viewpoints.

### What you need
Story books (see list below).

### What to do
Read the children a selection of stories that offer alternative views of the same event. The following may provide a useful starting point:
*The Pain and the Great One*, Judy Blume (1988) Pan
*The Picnic*, R. Brown (1992) Andersen Press
*My Mum and Our Dad*, Rose Impey (1992) Picture Puffin

Start a class discussion of stories like this. Encourage the children to read, discuss and retell the stories among themselves.

### Teaching content
Stories can be told from different viewpoints.

### What you need
Photocopiable pages 135, 136 and 137, scissors, glue, stapler, writing and drawing materials.

### What to do
The children should be well acquainted with the story of *Little Red Riding Hood*, but you may wish to begin the session either by reading

the story or by letting the children recall the events of the story orally to you.

Look first of all at the four pictures on the left-hand side of photocopiable page 135 and talk briefly with the children about what is happening in each of the pictures. Then ask them to look at the captions on the right-hand side and tell them that for each story a different character is writing the book. Pose the question: 'Who is telling the story?'

Look at each caption in turn – they are all written in the first person but who is writing each one? With the children, orally match up the author with the correct picture and discuss how we could have four different writers, Grandma, the Wolf, Red Riding Hood and her mother. Explain that you want the children to make up four different books, each one being told by a different writer, and show them the book 'covers' on photocopiable page 137. Explain the sequence of the activity.

• Cut out the pictures and captions from a copy of photocopiable page 135.

• Match together the correct picture and writer and paste them on to the blank grids on photocopiable page 136 (one grid for each matching picture and writer).

• Using a copy of photocopiable page 137, design a cover for each version, writing down which character wrote it.

• Finally, take their two completed sheets to you to be stapled.

This is an early stage in children's appreciation that a story can be written from different viewpoints. With older children, it may be useful to develop this idea and write a class book using the *Little Red Riding Hood* story, but with the Wolf telling the story. A great deal of oral work may be necessary to sequence the story, and role-play of the Wolf in a drama session may be particularly effective.

### Further development

*The Picnic*, R. Brown (1992) Andersen Press
*The Puppy who wanted a Boy*, J. Thayer (1991) Hippo Books
*Moving*, M. Rosen (1995) Picture Puffin

## 18

# OUR DAD/THOSE CHILDREN

### Teaching content

The same action can be described from different points of view.

### What you need

Photocopiable page 138, writing and drawing materials

### What to do

Put the children into pairs and give each pair a copy of photocopiable page 138. Ask one child in each pair to imagine that he or she is the father in the picture, and the other to imagine that he or she is one of the children.

Ask the children to write down exactly what their character is saying. Tell them not to discuss this, or show their partner, until they have finished.

Once they have finished, ask several children to share their writing with the whole class. Finally, ask them whether they can work in pairs to draw another situation in which the two characters hold very different viewpoints about what is going on. Display these on the wall or in a class book.

# GET LOST, LAURA!

# Get Lost, Laura!
### JENNIFER NORTHWAY

'Come and find us, Laura!' called Lucy.

Alice and Lucy argued and blamed each other.

Laura wanted to play. 'Get lost, Laura!' said Lucy.

Laura wasn't lost. She was sitting on Mum's knee all the time!

Lucy and Alice looked for Laura everywhere.

# THE HOUSE CAT

| | | |
|---|---|---|
| Tom-Cat lives in the whole house. | Home at last! | When the box is opened, Tom-Cat stretches and sniffs. This is not his house. |
| 'I will go home,' he says, and somehow he knows the way. | One day Mrs Spode-Fawcett squashes him into a cardboard box. | Tom-Cat must swim. He hates it. |

# MR PAM PAM AND THE HULLABAZOO

| It's true. | Mr Pam Pam and the baby came to visit. | Then one day in came the Hullabazoo with yellow hands and a green moustache. |
| Mr Pam Pam said, 'You'll never believe it, but every word I say is true... I saw a Hullabazoo.' | He said: 'I'm a Hullabazoo, nice to meet you.' | 'And it bounced... and it twizzled till it could twizzle no more.' |

# BLOOMING CATS

| Brave Nancy sees the old man slumped on the floor. | Every day the old man goes to feed the playground cats. | So Brave Nancy climbs the drainpipe. |
| --- | --- | --- |
| The old man is now better. He has lots of friends. | Then one morning the old man doesn't come. | The wacky woman chases the cats to the old man's house. |

# IF I MET...

◆ Write or draw what you would do. Write what you would say.

If I met the big bad wolf I would...

If I met the three bears I would...

If I met a giant I would...

If I met an ugly troll I would...

# UNTIDY ALEX 1

# UNTIDY ALEX 2

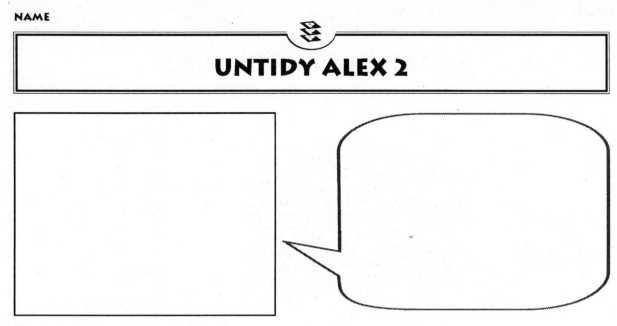

Draw your character here.

There is no room.

Alex is still untidy!

# WHAT HAPPENED NEXT?

an old lady rushed out
of her house shouting
'Help me!'

the twins came speeding
along the pavement on
their new roller-skates

a great big monster
jumped out from behind
a hedge

# WHAT HAPPENED NEXT?

and

_____
was walking along the
street quite happily
when...

# ONCE UPON A TIME

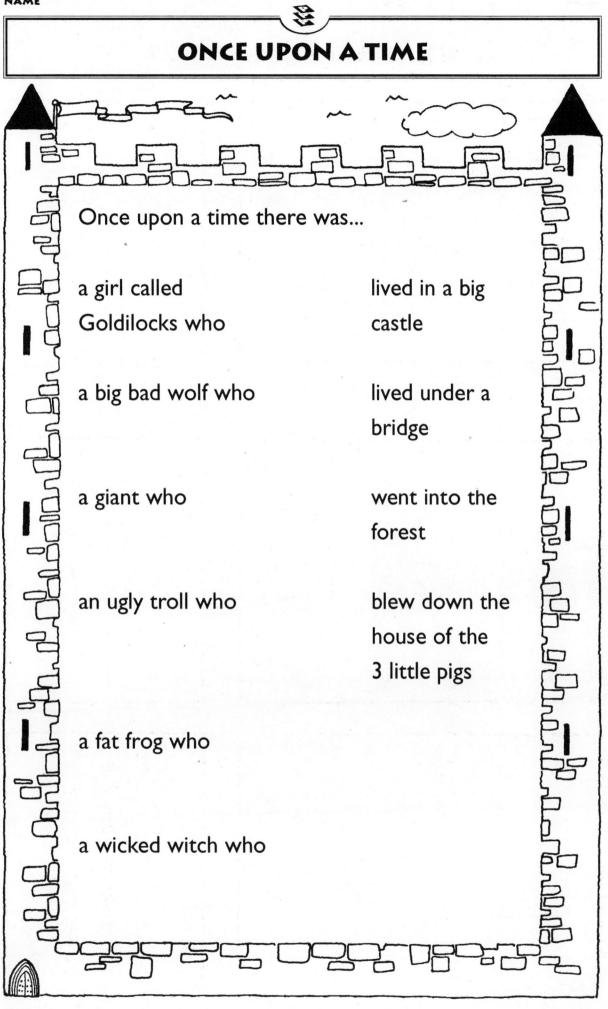

Once upon a time there was...

a girl called                           lived in a big
Goldilocks who                          castle

a big bad wolf who                      lived under a
                                        bridge

a giant who                             went into the
                                        forest

an ugly troll who                       blew down the
                                        house of the
                                        3 little pigs

a fat frog who

a wicked witch who

# WHAT DOES THE COVER TELL US?

Scholastic
IMAGINATIVE WRITING
Workshop

# WHAT DOES THE COVER TELL US?

◆ What was your present?

◆ When did you get it?

◆ What did you do with it?

# WHAT'S AT THE BOTTOM OF THE GARDEN?

# FIND A TITLE

Our story could be about:

Possible title

It might look like this...

# FIND A TITLE

# THE SCARIEST BOOK

In my grandma's house

there's a dark and dusty attic.

I never go there

on my own.

But one day

me and my friend Mick

took my little sister there

— to frighten her.

It was Mick's idea.

*from Jumble Joan by Rose Impey*

It was just mid-morning, but you would never have known it by the look in the sky. With each passing moment it grew darker and darker still. Great black clouds blew in and clashed and rumbled against one another overhead, quite chasing the sun from the sky in fright. And the old woman gathering wood in the forest below was, if truth be told, a little frightened herself.

*from The Lightning Bolt by Michael Bedard*

# WHAT *DID* HAPPEN?

Then she

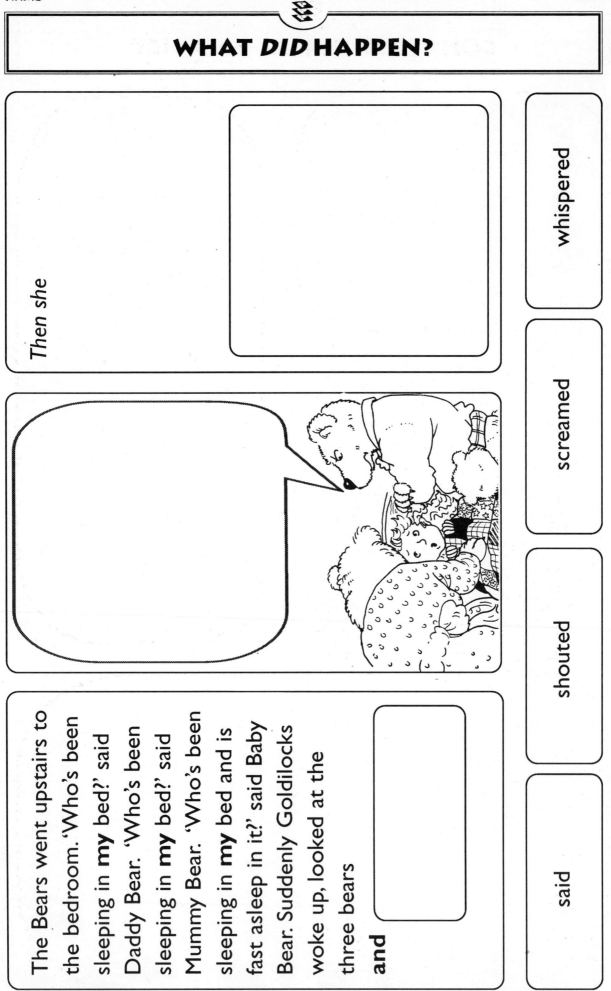

whispered

screamed

shouted

said

The Bears went upstairs to the bedroom. 'Who's been sleeping in **my** bed?' said Daddy Bear. 'Who's been sleeping in **my** bed?' said Mummy Bear. 'Who's been sleeping in **my** bed and is fast asleep in it?' said Baby Bear. Suddenly Goldilocks woke up, looked at the three bears **and**

# CONVERSATIONAL ENDINGS

# FAIRY-TALE ENDINGS

Cinderella and the prince got married and lived happily ever after.

'I'm so happy, I never thought I'd find you,' said the prince.
'Never mind,' said Cinderella. 'We can be together now for ever and ever.'

Cinderella and the prince stood in the garden, gazing into each other's eyes. The sky was blue and the birds were singing in the trees. They knew they would be happy from this day on.

NAME

# WHO IS TELLING THE STORY?

When I packed her basket and said, 'Now, off you go,' I had no idea what was going to happen.

I quickly changed into the old lady's clothes and jumped into bed.

Well, I looked at her mouth and thought Grandma's teeth don't usually look so big, so I said 'Grandma, what big teeth you've got!'

I was never so glad to see anyone in all my life. What a fright! And what a very dark cupboard.

# WHO IS TELLING THE STORY?

Scholastic
IMAGINATIVE WRITING
Workshop

# WHO IS TELLING THE STORY?

This is a book by

This book has been written by

This is my story by

I'll tell you my story by

# OUR DAD/THOSE CHILDREN

*Chapter Six*

# THE WRITING PROCESS

# INTRODUCTION

## What is the writing process approach?

The writing process has been framed in various ways. Donald Murray has suggested one of the most commonly used frameworks, identifying the following as key aspects: topic choice, rehearsal, drafting, revision and editing. (*Learning by Teaching* by D. Murray – Boyton, Cook, 1982)

The model is not supposed to represent a linear sequence of actions – in creating what Vygotsky called a 'web of meaning', writers move between considering the broad overview and focusing tightly on small aspects. (*Thought and Language* by L. S. Vygotsky – J. Wiley, 1962)

Topic choice and rehearsal involve thinking about possible ideas to choose topics and to decide the key events in the story. This may involve playing, daydreaming, sketching, making lists of words, reading or chatting with friends. In drafting, the writer makes a first attempt to write the story. Revision involves the writer rereading the work as a reader, changing and recasting to make it more effective. Editing involves making the final pre-publication changes, altering words, punctuation and layout to make the message clear and effective.

## Why is the writing process useful?

The process approach, with its emphasis on how and why young writers do what they do, provides a framework for thinking about storytelling and writing that is useful for both the teacher and the child.

It places the child, as a young author, firmly at the centre of the teaching focus. When teachers pay attention to the understandings that underpin the writing that children produce, they cannot help but teach more effectively and sympathetically. The more that a teacher notices about *how* a child crafts the story, the more closely and accurately he or she will be able to match her teaching to the child's needs.

The process approach identifies specific writing strategies and skills that children need to be shown and helped to use. Teaching writing thus becomes a case not of simply setting contexts and hoping for good results, but of introducing children, through modelling, discussion and collaborative work, to effective ways of working.

Through sharing stories and discussing the writing process, children develop a vocabulary for talking about writing and an awareness of what makes writing effective. They develop a framework for thinking about writing which allows them to notice distinctions, similarities and patterns in their own writing and in the work of others.

Such discussion enables children to become more effective writers and storytellers because it gives the child a sense of control and builds both a sense of authorship and an awareness of the learning process. Through discussion of writing and the writing process, children become more aware of what they know and can do as writers, more able to recognise, and take satisfaction in, what they have learned and the progress they have made.

## What can be problematic for young children?

Donald Murray's framework of the writing process is helpful, but infant teachers need to be clear about how it applies to working with young children.

Young children are undoubtedly enthusiastic storytellers, but their stories are often spoken, and not written down. Storytelling, rather than writing, allows the child to rely heavily on a host of external cues which help the child generate, structure and tell a story. The friend who interrupts enthusiastically with questions and new ideas, or the teacher who encourages with nods and gestures, both support the child in generating and sequencing the story by identifying possibilities within the story-line and giving immediate feedback about which bits are unclear, exciting or boring.

Moreover, in telling a story to a friend or a teacher, children can assume a shared understanding – they are aware of what the listeners know and can tailor their explanations to exploit this.

Writers cannot rely on this shared context or history. Instead, they must create the story inside their heads and, in telling it, imagine the reader and foresee the reader's reactions.

On top of this, children are often grappling with the symbol system of written language and must, unlike adults, think about how to form the letters and spell the words. The time, effort and attention required to physically write the story is another aspect which ensures that the writing process experienced by young children is significantly different from that of adults.

## Storytelling into writing – bridging the process for young children

Young children undoubtedly have important things to learn about creating stories in their heads and writing stories down.

Teachers can often help children by providing opportunities for them to create story-lines with friends, both through play and more structured activities. This provides an important forum for rehearsal – allowing children to explore and sequence ideas. By asking children to talk about and explain such stories, teachers are helping them to 'draft out' the story, recasting it for a more generalised audience that does not share the 'insider knowledge' of the players.

Often therefore, the processes of rehearsal and drafting may occur in places other than the writing session. Infant teachers can use their knowledge of the child and the integrated nature of the curriculum to sow the seeds for stories and allow them time and space to grow. To the untrained eye, stories carefully nurtured in this way may give the impression that story writing is a one-step process concerned primarily with getting the words on to a page. However, the teacher needs to recognise the importance of rehearsal and drafting, and plan opportunities for children to do this in class.

Young children do not always sustain a clear image of the reader. Children's attention is frequently focused on the telling of their story rather than on the story created in the reader's mind. This is not surprising. In the absence of a physical body giving instant and unequivocal feedback, the delight must lie in the telling rather than the audience response. Teachers need to be aware of this and ensure that children do see others reading and enjoying their stories. If children enjoy the experience of creating stories, of telling their stories and of seeing their stories recreated by the reader, they will develop into keen, expert and experienced storytellers and writers.

### Teaching the process

It goes without saying that the writing process cannot be taught without a classroom organisation and ethos that promotes and celebrates literacy, where children are confident and happy to see themselves as both authors and readers.

Even in such classrooms, however, discussion of process needs a light touch. Often the most effective teaching points about process are made in almost incidental ways. For example, the teacher who comments on *why* something was successful as well as noting that it was, is highlighting how the child might work in future and what makes writing effective. The teacher who explains *what* makes a story effective, or *why* he or she doesn't understand, is introducing a language for talking about writing and helping the child to envisage what the reader needs to know.

In short, comments that make the teacher's content/process framework explicit, empower the children to contribute to discussions about their work and thus create a powerful learning climate.

## CONTENTS AND ORGANISATION

The activities in this chapter have been written to raise awareness of the process of storytelling and writing, of how young children understand and use these processes and of how teachers can facilitate this understanding. The chapter is divided into four categories:

### Observing, organising and planning for writing

Teachers need to be aware of the range of opportunities for storytelling in school and at home. They need to consider how best to organise space, time, resources and teaching input to help children springboard from oral stories into writing. This section, therefore, is aimed specifically at the teacher. It contains audit and observation activities that will enable the teacher to reflect on and develop his or her own practice in order to ensure that the classroom environment facilitates children's writing.

### Opportunities for generating story topics and rehearsing stories

Authors need to develop an ability to recognise the story potential in different experiences and learn to exploit the situations that help them to develop these topics and ideas into story-lines. The activities in this short section raise children's awareness of where and when storytelling naturally happens, and of the sort of stories they like to tell.

### Moving into writing

The activities in this section focus on children writing stories: the frameworks they use, the conditions they need and how they feel about writing. They serve to help children identify aspects of the writing process, what makes a good story and the resources that can facilitate their work.

## Images of authorship and audience

Children need to perceive themselves as authors and to recognise authorship in others. Because the reader is a more distant audience than the listener, they also need to engage in these activities, which explicitly involve them in identifying the people who read their stories, in reading and responding to stories written by friends and in seeing others read and respond to their own stories.

| Activity | Teaching content | Star rating | Group size | Photo-copiable |
|---|---|---|---|---|
| **TEACHERS' ACTIVITIES** | | | | |
| 1 Where does story-making happen in the classroom? | Children make stories when playing with a range of different resources | n/a | n/a | n/a |
| 2 Building on children's experiences; links with writing | Using children's daily conversations for story-making and writing | | | |
| 3 Identifying what children know – review of observations | Recognising aspects of the writing process in talk and play | | | |
| 4 Teaching techniques – self-audit | Audit of ways used to teach writing | | | |
| 5 Setting up and developing a writing area | Organisation for writing | | | |
| 6 What's available in the classroom to motivate children to write? | Using resources to motivate children to write | | | |
| 7 Where does children's writing go? | Ensuring a range of audiences for writing | | | |
| **CHILDREN'S ACTIVITIES** | | | | |
| 1 Night-time stories | Stories we tell ourselves can be written for others | * | 1↷2 | |
| 2 Stories, stories everywhere (but which could I use best?) | Awareness of the range of stories children enjoy hearing and writing | ** | 1 | ✓ |
| 3 Favourite writing places | Optimum conditions for writing | */*** | 1 | |
| 4 My first story | Emotional investment in writing; awareness of progression in scribing | **/*** | 1 | |
| 5 What I like best about writing is... | Aspects of the writing process; identifying own strengths | **/*** | 1↷2 | ✓ |
| 6 Feelings about writing | Emotions towards writing | *** | Ⓦ↷2 | |
| 7 How has your writing improved? | Ingredients for a good story; awareness of progress in writing | *** | 1 | |
| 8 Storytellers I have known | Storytelling is fun and everyone does it | */*** | 1 | |
| 9 Important people, important opinions | Writing stories gives others pleasure | */*** | 1 | |
| 10 The writer's wall | Responding to writing; awareness of audience | **/*** | Ⓦ↷1 | ✓ |
| 11 Critical friends | Responding to writing | **/*** | 2/4/Ⓦ | ✓ |
| 12 Poster adverts | Identifying audience; identifying strengths of a story | **/*** | 1 | |
| 13 Where do my stories go? | Who reads the stories written by children? | *** | 1/2 | ✓ |

A = photocopiable anthology page
Ⓦ = whole group

## WHERE DOES STORY-MAKING HAPPEN IN THE CLASSROOM?

*When are children making stories?* From a very early age, children make their own stories naturally through play situations and everyday experiences. Although these are being created in the mind and orally in interaction with others, the teacher needs to be aware of what children enjoy talking about and could make into stories. There may be nothing written or scribed, but this is a very necessary stage in which children rehearse the stories that can lead to writing at a later stage.

### Stories in the classroom: children talking to children

It may be useful to observe small groups of children at selected activity/choosing/free/directed play times, and to focus on:
• What kinds of stories are they creating?
• What do they know about characterisation/setting/structure?
• What helps them to make stories:
  – the materials/props provided?
  – interaction with each other?
  – interaction with you or other adults?

Listen to what they say and what they do. You may be surprised at what you hear! There may be other questions which you could add to the list.

Use this grid to note your initial observations on the above questions as you watch children at play.

| POSSIBLE PLAY EXPERIENCES | OBSERVATIONAL NOTES |
|---|---|
| **Imaginative areas**<br>home corner / café / hairdresser's / the Three Bears' cottage / spaceship / hospital / garden centre / fantasy castle / travel agency / toy shop / bookshop / post office... | |
| **Construction materials**<br>large bricks / small bricks / LEGO / DUPLO / Mobilo... | |
| **'Small world' toys**<br>zoo / farm / play people / floor mats / garage / house / dinosaurs... | |
| **Creative activities**<br>painting / collage / model making / drawings / Plasticine pictures | |
| **Baking / Cooking**<br>Planning a party / Teddy Bears' picnic... | |
| **Display tables**<br>shells / 'our favourite toys' / shiny things / jewellery... | |
| **Puppets**<br>flannelgraphs to create stories / background pictures | |

# HOW CAN I BUILD UPON CHILDREN'S EXPERIENCE AND HELP THEM TO MAKE LINKS WITH WRITING?

In addition to the variety of story-making opportunities which may arise through child-initiated and adult-led play experiences, there are other routines within the school day and directed activities which can provide opportunities for story-making.

Below is a list of some further opportunities. Tick whether you currently use these situations. Consider ways in which you could use them to enhance children's story-making and story-writing skills and their understanding of the processes involved.

| Situation / Activity / Context | ✓ | How could I develop this? |
|---|---|---|
| Listening to children's 'play' stories<br>News time – personal stories | | |
| Show and tell / Our table of things we have brought to talk about | | |
| Planning stories, eg. 'What are you going to do in the cafe today? What will you need?' | | |
| Greeting children at the beginning of the day, eg. 'Did you go to your gran's house last night? What did you do?' | | |
| Saying goodbye at the end of the day, eg. 'I hope you enjoy the party. Remember to tell us all about it tomorrow.' | | |
| Playtimes/lunchtimes | | |
| Using photographs | | |
| A story 'postbox' – I've got a story to tell | | |
| Blank book beside the area to share with other children, eg. The models we've made; Today in the spaceship; Every picture tells a story; Down on the farm. | | |

# IDENTIFYING WHAT CHILDREN KNOW – REVIEW OF OBSERVATIONS

Look back at the notes you made for the observation tasks in Activity 2 and tick the processes involved in the children's story-making. There are some examples beside each one. You could add others from your observations.

| | | |
|---|---|---|
| **Plan a story** | | Let's have a party for the bears.<br>I'm going to make a rocket that goes to the moon. |
| **Organise a sequence of events** | | We'll make a castle, then put some flags on the top. |
| **Take on roles** | | I'll be the Baby Bear and you can be Goldilocks. |
| **Interact with others in role** | | You can't come in here again because you broke my chair! |
| **Recognise setting/time** | | My dinosaurs lived in a forest a long, long time ago. |
| **Engage in dialogue** | | 'I'd like to go on holiday please.'<br>'Where do you want to go to?'<br>'I want to go on an aeroplane.'<br>'A big aeroplane or a little one?' |
| **Carry the story forward** | | Look at the mess in our toy shop! It must have been burglars. Let's phone the police. Don't touch anything until they come. |
| **Adopt the voice of a character** | | I'll huff and I'll puff and I'll blow your house down! |
| **'Review' the story** | | I liked the bit when you said 'Who's been sitting on my chair?' |
| **Link to everyday experiences** | | When my mum makes cakes... |
| **Make links to the past** | | When I had my party... |

# TEACHING TECHNIQUES – SELF-AUDIT

There are many ways in which children can be helped to develop their writing. Teachers have a wide repertoire of approaches and tasks that offer different types of support. This activity will enable teachers to ascertain how frequently different techniques are used and identify some of the benefits of each.

| | List children who would benefit from this. | How often do I do this? | When could I do this? |
|---|---|---|---|
| **Modelling the writing process** Useful for: Introducing children to ways of thinking and doing; the way writers work; the type of decisions writers make; what the product might look like. | | | |
| **Scribing** Useful for: Recording children's ideas and stories quickly; to let them concentrate on the content/ideas; showing/discussing how letters and words are formed (and why); getting a quick and well-presented end-product. | | | |
| **Emergent writing** Useful for: Noticing and using what children know and can do; developing confidence and ownership. | | | |
| **Paired writing** Useful for: Building confidence and enthusiasm; encouraging independence; supporting content/ideas and secretarial skills. | | | |
| **Writing friends** Useful for: Building confidence, enthusiasm and purpose; developing audience awareness. | | | |
| **Writing at home with parents/family** Useful for: Confidence, emotional support, enthusiasm, topic choice and development. | | | |

# HOW COULD I SET UP AND DEVELOP A WRITING AREA?

Before considering this question it would be useful to decide:

### Why am I doing it?

What are the purposes/outcomes I hope to achieve? For example:
• raise the profile of 'writing';
• develop children's confidence;
• enable children to see themselves as writers;
• make links to other areas and experiences.

### Where will it be?

Is there space available to create an area within the room? If so, will it be located next to the book corner to enable children to make links with other aspects of language? If there is not sufficient space, could you use a writing 'box' with materials inside, which may be more flexible and could be located in different parts of the room?

### What will it contain?

In developing an area, you may decide to begin with limited resources and build upon these as children use the area more frequently, ask for specific materials or are introduced to different stimuli which are noted later in the chapter. Is there sufficient space for a table and chairs? How many children could 'write' there?

Begin with a variety of paper, pencils and some felt-tipped pens or crayons. All of these should be carefully labelled within the area to enable children to collect and return materials to their appropriate place.

If the area can be located next to wall space, this would create an ideal opportunity to display children's stories within the area, show the value of their work and enable the sharing of ideas.

### When and how will it be used?

There may be a variety of times within the day when children could work in the area or use the resources available:
• in a free-choice activity;
• as part of a work programme or series of tasks;
• after discussion of a 'story' with another child/teacher/class;
• in rotation after a 'choosing time' to draw the activities in which they were involved.

They may also use the areas independently, with a friend, or collaboratively as a small group.

In establishing an area for the first time, you will have to make time to observe how it is being used to inform future planning and organisation of the resources within it.

# WHAT'S AVAILABLE IN THE CLASSROOM TO MOTIVATE CHILDREN TO WRITE?

Very often, the resources available to children can motivate them to write. Look at the variety suggested here.

blank books

clipboards

envelopes

art materials

a variety of pens and pencils

paper in different shapes, sizes and colours

pictures to stimulate children's thinking and provide story 'starts'

telephones to promote dialogue

story tapes and blank tapes onto which children can record their own stories

newspapers to enable children to look at the layout of stories

computers for children to word-process their own stories

a selection of books

Once upon a time...
word banks/lists of words

Memo:
memos, written by you or the children, about the books you have read

letters written by the children about their favourite stories

# WHERE DOES CHILDREN'S WRITING GO?

What do you do with children's writing when
they have finished?
Here is a list of some possibilities. Consider
your present practice using this list and tick
what you do usually/sometimes/never.

| | usually | sometimes | never |
|---|---|---|---|
| in a jotter or exercise book | ☐ | ☐ | ☐ |
| on a wall in the classroom | ☐ | ☐ | ☐ |
| in the corridor | ☐ | ☐ | ☐ |
| on a wall specially designated for writing, for example 'We are writers'. | ☐ | ☐ | ☐ |
| presented to another class | ☐ | ☐ | ☐ |
| presented at an assembly | ☐ | ☐ | ☐ |
| to a friend | ☐ | ☐ | ☐ |
| to the nursery | ☐ | ☐ | ☐ |
| to the headteacher's room | ☐ | ☐ | ☐ |
| shared at a together/story time | ☐ | ☐ | ☐ |
| on video | ☐ | ☐ | ☐ |
| in their personal record of achievement | ☐ | ☐ | ☐ |
| in a frame (bordered or other) | ☐ | ☐ | ☐ |
| in the book area | ☐ | ☐ | ☐ |
| in the writing area | ☐ | ☐ | ☐ |
| to someone as a special present | ☐ | ☐ | ☐ |
| photocopied to include in class books | ☐ | ☐ | ☐ |
| photocopied as a 'story to swap' with other children | ☐ | ☐ | ☐ |

Are there ideas from this list that you may try out?

Are there any that you may add to the list?

**Other questions to consider**

Do children know what happens to their writing?

Do children have any choice in what happens to their writing?

How do you consult them?

# OPPORTUNITIES FOR GENERATING STORY TOPICS AND REHEARSING STORIES

## 1

## NIGHT-TIME STORIES

### Teaching content
We all tell stories to ourselves. Stories can occur at any time. Sometimes the stories we tell ourselves can also be interesting to others.

### What you need
Writing materials (including different-sized paper.)

### What to do
Ask the children to describe what happens when they go to bed at night. Try to move from the familiar routines of washing and the brushing of teeth to the point at which they are lying in the dark, waiting for sleep. What are the night-time thoughts that run through their heads? Do they think about things that happened during the day; the games they played; things they did; the people they met; or perhaps their toys; or the things they plan to do tomorrow?

Give each child a sheet of A4 paper and ask the children to draw *one* thing that they thought about last night. Put the class into pairs and give them an opportunity to explain their drawings to each other before asking a few pairs to share their stories with the whole class.

Make sure that the children are very clear that these are stories and that night dreams are a good source of ideas for writing stories.

Explain that the stories can be told briefly, or that they can be told at much greater length. Suggest making a 'Night-time story book'. Show the children a selection of paper of different sizes and allow them to choose whether to tell their own story for the 'Night-time story book' in a sentence or at much greater length.

## 2

## STORIES, STORIES EVERYWHERE (BUT WHICH COULD I USE BEST?)

### Teaching content
Awareness of the range of stories children enjoy and write, using previous experiences for their writing.

### What you need
Photocopiable page 156, writing materials.

### What to do
Brainstorm with the class or group all the stories they have written over the past few months. Categorise the brainstorm into topics such as stories about: home, school, animals, adventures, funny stories, true stories, magical stories and so on.

Give each child a copy of photocopiable page 156 and ask the children to think about which types of stories arise easily from the situations detailed on the sheet. Then discuss whether they have ever used, or thought of using, ideas or whole stories from these situations in their writing. Ask the children to cross out situations that they think would never generate ideas for a written story in school and to put a star beside those that could often lead to writing a story.

Discussion of this with both individuals and the class can yield information about the children's interests and experiences in story-making, as well as encouraging the children to become aware of the range of stories they write and showing them how to draw from a range of experiences for ideas for their writing.

### 3

## FAVOURITE WRITING PLACES

### Teaching content

Raising awareness of when children write and their optimum conditions for writing.

### What you need

Writing and drawing materials.

### What to do

Talk to the children about the different places in which they write, in school and at home. You may like to describe some of the places that you like (or do not like) to work in. At home, do the children ever write or draw? Do they have their own writing/drawing materials and, if so, where do they keep them? If not, whose do they use? Do the children have their own writing/drawing table at home? Do they like to write in bed; in their bedroom; at the kitchen table or in a room with the family all around them?

Discussion about where children like writing in school can also be interesting: do they like writing in the classroom or outside the classroom? Do they like to be surrounded by others also writing? Do they like the classroom to be quiet or busy while they are writing? Does *what* they are writing make a difference?

When children have had plenty of opportunity to contribute to the discussion, ask them to draw a picture of their favourite place for writing and to write an explanatory sentence beneath it. These individual contributions can be made into a class book.

### 4

## MY FIRST STORY

### Teaching content

Awareness of development in scribing skills; writing stories down.

### What you need

No resources needed.

### What to do

Begin by asking the children about their younger brothers and sisters. What sort of things do they like to do? Do they enjoy telling stories, or making up stories with others? Do they ever write stories, or pretend to write stories?

Can the children remember when they first started to tell stories? Can they remember the earliest story they wrote, or asked someone to write down? What was it about? What did they think after the story? What did others say about the story and how did this make them feel?

Suggest to the children that if they enjoyed writing and telling stories when they were younger, and if they benefited from the encouragement of their family, that other young children might also appreciate such encouragement. Ask the children to identify *one* younger child who they could encourage to tell a story and maybe they could offer to write and illustrate the story for them. Emphasise that it could be a story about something that happened at home, in play, on an outing or at an event.

### 5

## WHAT I LIKE BEST ABOUT WRITING IS...

### Teaching content

Aspects of the writing process, identification of own strengths.

### What you need

Photocopiable page 157, writing materials, paper and squares for class bar graph, chalkboard.

### What to do

Read through photocopiable page 157 with the children. Explain that each child on the photocopiable sheet has a different view of what they like about writing and why. Can the children think of any things they like about writing not depicted on the sheet? List these on the board.

Give each child a copy of photocopiable page 157 and ask the children to think about all the statements. Tell the children to select the one that reflects what they like *best* about

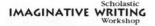

writing. If they like something *not* listed on the photocopiable sheet, they can write it on the back of the sheet.

Now, put the children into pairs and ask them to compare what they like best about writing and discuss why. Choose some pairs to talk to the class about their choices. Finally, tell the children to cut out the illustrated statement they have selected and display these as a class bar graph.

## FEELINGS ABOUT WRITING

### Teaching content
Awareness of emotions and stages of the writing process.

### What you need
Writing materials, chalkboard.

### What to do
Remind the children of the last story they wrote by asking them to recall briefly what it was about and when/where they wrote it.

Explain that sometimes people enjoy writing more than at other times. Ask the children to think about how much they enjoyed writing their last story and to give an honest reaction. Who enjoyed writing it? Who partly enjoyed

writing it? Who didn't enjoy writing it?

If you think that many of the children will simply make a response to please you, ask the children to discuss their reactions in pairs and to indicate their response in the form of a show of hands.

Explain that writers often have different reactions to stories they have written. Working in pairs, ask the children to discuss their own stories and the feelings they have had during the writing process. They may have felt excited, impatient, busy, calm, worried, cross or dreamy. Write some headings on the board to provide the children with a format for their discussion:
• When the teacher first suggested writing a story, I felt...
• When I started thinking, talking or drawing about the story, I felt...
• When I began writing the story, I felt...
• When I was in the middle, I felt...
• When I finished, I felt...
• When I talked about my story, I felt...

## HOW HAS YOUR WRITING IMPROVED?

### Teaching content
Ingredients for a good story; progress in writing.

### What you need
Writing materials.

### What to do
With the class, brainstorm all the things that they think teachers, parents and other children look for when reading a piece of writing. This may raise issues such as whether the children think that teachers look for something different from their peers.

Ask the children to select the three or four aspects of writing that they think are most important and to write about them on a sheet of A4 paper, indicating for each aspect how good they think they are at it and whether they think they have improved recently. Tell the children to give their sheet a heading 'The most important things about writing my stories'. Children's choices and their reasons for them can become the basis for informal discussion, as can their self-assessments of progress and achievement.

## 8

## STORYTELLERS I HAVE KNOWN

### Teaching content
Adults tell stories too; storytelling is fun.

### What you need
Writing and drawing/painting materials.

### What to do
Tell the children that many adults enjoy telling and writing stories. Many children will be able to remember the stories their parents invented to entertain them when they were in their pre-school years. Some will still be told invented stories on a regular basis – to keep them quiet on car or bus journeys, for example.

Ask the children to draw, or to paint, a picture of *one* adult they know who is a good storyteller. Ask them to write a short sentence to explain who the person is and what (or who) he or she tells good stories about. They may also like to say why they like the stories. The pictures and the written work can be made into a wall display.

### Further development
Suggest that the children ask the adult storyteller to write down their story so that it can be read. Remind the children that some adults are busy and may not have time, but that they could help by offering to start the story off or to draw the pictures to illustrate it.

## 9

## IMPORTANT PEOPLE, IMPORTANT OPINIONS

### Teaching content
Other people read the children's stories with enjoyment.

### What you need
A story chosen by the child, which he or she has recently written, A3 and A4 paper, chalkboard, writing and drawing materials.

### What to do
Talk to the class about all the people who are important to them and record their suggestions as a list on the board. The list may include family members at home – either children or adults – family members who live some distance

away, neighbours, babysitters, friends and so on.

Ask the children to each pick three people who are particularly important to them and to draw or paint each person. The drawings should be large enough so that when cut out, all three will fit on to an A3 sheet of paper.

Explain that opinions matter when people are important to us. Suggest that the children choose one story which they have recently written (one that they think they have written well) and read it to each of the people they have drawn. Tell the children to ask each adult to write a brief note stating which part of the story he or she liked best and whether he or she would like to hear or see other stories written by the child.

## 10

## THE WRITER'S WALL

### Teaching content

Evaluating other people's writing will help each individual to become more aware of authorship in general and of what makes effective writing. Experience of publication will help children to be more aware of writing for an audience.

### What you need

Wall space to display individual pieces of writing, photocopiable page 158, card, boxes of evaluation forms (cereal box with front cut out, covered in coloured paper and an example of the evaluation form stuck on the front), postbox for completed evaluations, writing materials.

### What to do

Tell the children that you would like them to select pieces of their writing to display on the wall for others to read. The children can do one of the following:

• choose a piece of their own writing which they think is the best;

• ask their writing partner to read two or three pieces of writing and discuss with them which one to select;

• discuss with you which piece to select.

After setting up the wall display, you may want to allow children to mount and display their chosen piece of work. Write a heading for

the display entitled 'The writer's wall: Please read our stories'.

Once the pieces have been displayed, show the children a copy of the Writer's Wall Evaluation Sheet on photocopiable page 158 and read through the questions. Explain that these forms will be available on the table underneath the wall display and that children in the class, other children in the school, staff, parents or visitors will all be able to fill in the forms, saying what they liked about the writing.

At the end of the week, empty the comments box and read the children the comments people have made. Periodically, you could add some flash cards, displaying chosen comments, to the display.

Encourage the children to select new pieces for comment so that the wall continues to display recent writing. All children's work should be displayed over a period of time.

## 11

## CRITICAL FRIENDS

### Teaching content

Evaluating other people's writing will help each individual to become more aware of authorship in general and of what makes effective writing. Experience of publication will help children to be more aware of writing for an audience.

### What you need
Photocopiable page 159, writing materials.

### What to do
Group the children into pairs so that each child is paired with someone he or she would like to share their writing with. Tell the children to choose a piece of writing that they would like their partner to read and comment on. Then discuss the 'Critical friends' evaluation sheet on photocopiable page 159 and check that the children understand what they are being asked at each point. Let the children know that each partner will use the form to make a report to the class or group about his or her friend's piece of writing. This activity can be carried out on a number of occasions with different pieces of writing.

## POSTER ADVERTS

### Teaching content
Identifying audience; identifying strengths of a story.

### What you need
Identification of one successful story that each child has written, writing and drawing/painting materials.

### What to do
Talk to the children about the stories which they have written in the past. Ask them about stories they have written in school, at home, with friends and alone.

Ask them to each think of *one* story they have written in the past that makes them feel really proud. What was it called? What was it about?

Ask the children to imagine that they are illustrators and to design a poster to advertise this story. While they work, encourage the children to think about the story and:
• who would like to read it;
• what they particularly like about it;
• what special qualities it has;
• how they feel about others reading it.

Display the posters on the wall, along with a display of the stories. Encourage the children to talk about their stories to each other.

## WHERE DO MY STORIES GO?

### Teaching content
Who reads the stories written by children?

### What you need
Photocopiable page 160, writing materials, chalkboard.

### What to do
Begin the lesson by talking to the children about stories and what a writer can do with them once they have been written. Tell them about some of the stories you have written, either recently or when you were at school, and what you liked to do with them: did you show them or give them to friends; take them home to show your parents; put them on the wall; put them into a book of stories; put them in a special place (perhaps in your bedroom); or did the stories stay at school? If so, were you happy about this, or did you wish for an alternative destination?

Give each child a copy of photocopiable page 160 and work through the options given in the picture at the top of the sheet. Help the children to remember the last few stories they have written (list these on the board if necessary) and ask them to write the titles of the stories on a sheet of paper. Then ask the children to draw a star or put a tick next to the picture which shows what happened to each of the stories they have listed. If there isn't a drawing of a destination they require, tell the children to write it on the separate sheet on which they have written the titles of their stories. Finally, ask them to answer the two questions on the photocopiable sheet and complete the sentence that begins 'The nicest thing that ever happened to my writing was...'

Photocopiable page 160 provides an interesting focus for discussion and reflection. It serves to make both children and teacher more aware of what can happen to stories, but also to make children aware that they can make choices about what to do with their stories – that they can ask to take a story home to show parents, or to copy a story for a wall display or into book format for the class library. (Word-processing offers much potential for this.)

# STORIES, STORIES EVERYWHERE

# WHAT I LIKE BEST ABOUT WRITING IS...

someone reading my story

thinking of the story ideas

talking about the story with friends

writing it down

reading through my own finished story

illustrating the story

talking with the teacher about the story

telling my mum/dad about the story

# WRITER'S WALL EVALUATION SHEET

◆ Please read our writing and choose some pieces of writing you like. We want to know **what you like about them**, so please write down the title of the story and the author's name, and tick the answers or write your own comments in the box.

Title:

Author:

I liked this story because:

something really interesting happens ☐

something funny happens ☐

something exciting happens ☐

something sad happens ☐

| comments |
| --- |
| |

I liked this setting because it was:

scary ☐     magical ☐     happy ☐     realistic ☐

| comments |
| --- |
| |

I liked this character because he/she was:

| funny ☐ | sad ☐ | fantastic ☐ | magical ☐ |
| --- | --- | --- | --- |
| realistic ☐ | old ☐ | young ☐ | wicked ☐ |
| like someone I know ☐ | just like me ☐ | | |

| comments |
| --- |
| |

# CRITICAL FRIENDS

◆ Read your friend's writing carefully. Tell your friend and other people in the class what you liked best about the writing. This sheet has some ideas to help you and a space at the bottom to write down what you liked best.

Title:

Author:

Sometimes people like stories because something really interesting happens, there is a character they really enjoy or it has:

- ◆ a good title
- ◆ a good beginning
- ◆ a good ending
- ◆ a good setting
- ◆ good pictures

I liked this story because

# WHERE DO MY STORIES GO?

◆ Where would *you* most like your writing to go?



◆ Where should your writing *never* go?



◆ The nicest thing that ever happened to my writing was

*Chapter Seven*

# USING THE STORY BOOKS

| Activity | Teaching content | Star rating | Group size | Photo-copiable |
|---|---|---|---|---|
| **KNOCK KNOCK WHO'S THERE?** | | | | |
| 1 Who's behind the door? | Prediction and repetition as structural devices | */** | 4 | ✓ |
| 2 If you come in here | Dialogue to reveal character's feelings | */** | 2 | ✓A |
| 3 Funny feet and fitting shoes | Characters need appropriate clothes | * | (W)⇨1 | |
| 4 Where I live | Settings can indicate character | * | 2 | |
| **BLOOMING CATS** | | | | |
| 1 Words, pictures and layout | Settings evoke mood. Layout affects how the story is read | ** | 4 | ✓ |
| 2 Another title, another story | The title reflects the story and is chosen by the author | ** | 2 | |
| 3 Dedications | Authors are real people with families | ** | 1 | |
| 4 First and last | Detail in settings creates the mood. Endings need to resolve the story | ** | 1 | A |
| 5 Cat talk | Characterisation through action and speech | ** | 1 | ✓ |
| **SCARY STORY** | | | | |
| 1 My own scary story | Front cover can indicate the type of story | */** | (W)⇨1 | |
| 2 Eyes everywhere! | Facial expression indicates feelings | */** | (W)⇨2⇨1 | ✓ |
| 3 If I *met* the scary ghost... | Characters react in different ways | */** | (W)⇨1 | ✓ |
| 4 If I *was* the scary ghost... | Stories can be told from different viewpoints | */** | (W)⇨2 | |
| 5 In the torchlight | Detail and focus can create atmosphere | */** | (W)⇨2 | ✓ |
| 6 Safe at last? | Possible turning points and endings for stories | */** | (W)⇨1 | ✓ |
| **GET LOST, LAURA!** | | | | |
| 1 Our story about Laura | Stories can be reviewed, changed and created | */** | 4 | |
| 2 When I was little | Characterisation through action, speech and appearance | */** | (W)⇨1 | ✓ |
| 3 Lost! Stories of the search | Stories take place in different settings | */** | (W)⇨1 | |
| 4 I don't like it when others tell me... | Speech and dialogue can indicate emotions | */** | (W)⇨1 | ✓ |
| **THE GARDEN** | | | | |
| 1 She had never seen anything quite like it before... | Vocabulary selection for short but vivid description of settings | *** | 4⇨1 | |
| 2 From the centre to the edge | Viewpoint to structure a description | **/*** | 2 | |
| 3 Night sky/morning sky | Vocabulary to evoke mood and detail of setting | *** | 2 | |
| 4 A dream | People build different images of scenes in stories | **/*** | (W)⇨1⇨2 | |
| 5 The original American people | Using settings to accentuate character | *** | 1/2 | |
| **THE HOUSE CAT** | | | | |
| 1 The way home | Short direct phrases increase the pace of the story | **/*** | (W)⇨2 | ✓ |
| 2 Snapshots of school | Structure and detail for descriptions | **/*** | (W)⇨1 | |
| 3 Could I find my way home? | Different characters notice different aspects of setting | **/*** | (W)⇨1⇨2 | |
| 4 The reflection in your eyes | Characterisation through action | **/*** | (W)⇨1 | |
| **RUBY** | | | | |
| 1 Ruby is an interesting bear | Making characters different makes them more interesting | */** | 4⇨2 | |
| 2 What kind of bear is Ruby? | Thoughts, speech and actions indicate character | */** | (W)⇨1 | ✓ |
| 3 My special toy | Name, appearance and history indicate certain aspects | * | (W)⇨2 | |
| 4 Escape | Telling the story from different viewpoints | */** | 2 | |
| **MR PAM PAM** | | | | |
| 1 Food for a king; food for Mr Pam Pam | Characterisation through speech | ** | (W)⇨2 | |
| 2 Pam Pam knocking on your door! | Characterisation through speech and action | ** | (W)⇨2 | ✓ |
| 3 The storytellers | The stories people tell reflect character | ** | 1⇨2 | ✓ |
| 4 Pam Pam looking for new clothes! | Characterisation through dress and appearance | */** | 1 | |
| 5 Moving like a Hullabazoo | Vocabulary to describe movement | ** | 1⇨(W) | |

A = photocopiable anthology page   (W) = whole group

# INTRODUCTION

### Why the story books are important

The story books have been included in the *Writing Workshop* for a variety of reasons.

• *Developing concepts of authorship.* The story books are important because they give the children a common model through which they can examine both the structure and the language choices authors make. This discussion helps children to understand that authors make choices; each book provides an example of the way in which one author has decided to tell the story.

• *Developing reading–writing links.* Reading and discussing the books also helps the children to read like writers, to take an insider's view of reading and writing in which they recognise and appreciate the decisions the author has to make and how he or she has chosen to craft the story.

• *Developing knowledge about language; a language for talking about stories.* Recent curricular initiatives have emphasised the importance of knowledge about language and genre. Children need to develop a language for talking about language and literacy, but they need to do this for real purposes. Discussion of the books helps to build up a language for talking about stories and about particular aspects of stories. It provides a real context in which children quite simply need the vocabulary to explain what they notice and mean. Because the children are using the vocabulary and concepts for real communicative purposes, the learning is meaningful and powerful – it changes the way in which they think and view the world.

• *Developing conscious knowledge about writing.* When learners acquire knowledge about how authors create particular effects, not only do they understand how writing works, but they begin to think that they could do this too. They begin to acquire understanding of the strategies and techniques in a conscious way. Because it changes their thinking, it changes and informs the way in which they view their own writing.

### Why this selection of books?

The books have been selected to provide a range of different types of stories and a variety of styles of illustration and layout. They will appeal to children of different ages, although, as with all good books, they can be read with different levels of sophistication; the more a reader knows, the more insight he or she brings to both the interpretation of the story – the motivation of characters, implications of the setting and so on – and the skill of the writer.

The activities related to the story books provide a context for children to investigate how aspects of characterisation, setting, structure and process combine in one published story. Particular aspects explored within each story-context are summarised on the chart on page 162. Star ratings indicate the approximate level of difficulty of each story in terms of its content and interest level. Within some activities there are suggestions for providing more support or challenge to enable the teacher to differentiate within a class. Brief descriptors at the start of each book-context explain the focus of the activities in terms of the aspects of writing they target.

## Reading the books to the children

If children are to enjoy reading and writing, they must enjoy stories. In early experiences, children need time and opportunity to simply listen to the story and live it 'inside their heads'. Familiarity and enthusiasm with the story are necessary precursors to any discussion or exploration of how the story has been told.

When the books are shared with children, aspects of the writer's craft can be highlighted naturally and in context simply by reading the story well. The way that a story is read can ensure children want to look at the pictures, and encourage them to think about the characters, the setting and the implications that small details may have for the plot.

## Introducing and using the books

The books can be introduced to the children in a number of different ways by the teacher:
• discussing the front-cover illustration and the title, thereby helping children to tune into the story and also raising their awareness of authorship (each book was written by a real, live person);
• introducing the story as the class 'book of the week';
• asking a particular child or group of children to read the story, or to listen to it on tape, and tell the teacher (or class) their opinion or response to the story;
• telling the children about the main character and promising them that the story about this character will be read to them the next day;
• reading the book to the children and telling them how much he or she enjoyed it;
• putting the book in the book area for children to choose.

The introduction to each set of book-based activities contains specific suggestions about how the books may be used with the class.

## Using the tape

The tape has been produced to support and extend the use of the stories in the classroom. It enhances, rather than replaces, the role of the teacher, allowing children to both revisit and enjoy the stories at their own pace. As mentioned in the introduction to this book, children can choose to listen to the tape as individuals, with groups of friends or within specified work groups. Teachers may thus use the tapes to generate enthusiasm and interest, or as a basis for more focused examination of the text. As part of a work programme, the tapes enable particular groups or individuals to remember and revise the stories before key activities, or as a follow-up to those activities, allowing space and time for reflection upon them.

The style of the story readings illustrates how stories are interpreted according to their content and will influence the mind-pictures which the children create. Teachers will probably find it useful to listen to a chosen story on tape prior to reading it to the class, in order to help make explicit links between the way the story is read and the illustrations, layout and segmentation of the story.

# KNOCK KNOCK WHO'S THERE?

*Knock Knock Who's There?* by Sally Grindley and Anthony Browne tells the story of a knock knock game played between a father and daughter at bedtime. There is a tension throughout the narrative because of its unexpected nature. This has the effect of children finding it scary. The story is structured by the knock knock game and introduces a different imaginary character in reply to each knock knock question. Clues to who the character behind the door might be are contained in the changing pattern of the wallpaper and parts of the character seen behind the door which is slightly ajar. However, every character seems to be wearing Daddy's slippers, revealing the fact that in reality it is Daddy every time. The story draws on children's knowledge of fairy-tale characters. The simple repetitive structure, and the opportunity for participation and for prediction, make this an enjoyable story for younger children.

The children will quickly become familiar with the story and will enjoy listening to it repeatedly on the story tape. Familiarity developed by listening to the tape will then help them to appreciate the way in which the author has used a repetitive structure, supported by clear illustrations (providing clues) and short, simple text, to craft an appealing story.

Read the entire story to small groups of children, showing the pictures at each point. This will enable all of the children to examine the picture clues and encourage them to predict *who* might be behind the door on each occasion. Let the book be available for children to refer to during the writing activities.

## About the author and illustrator

Sally Grindley has written many children's books. Her story *The Boy who wanted to be King* was shown on Granada TV in 1986. She is the Editorial Director of Books for Children Book Club, and was a judge for the Mother Goose Award for the most promising newcomer to children's book illustration (sponsored by Books for Children). She has three sons and lives in Gloucestershire. Her hobbies include collecting hand-made wooden toys, and Noah's Ark books and artefacts.

Anthony Browne, a Kate Greenaway Award and Kurt Maschler Award winner, is an established and popular author/artist of books for children. He spent much of his childhood drawing and painting, and following school went on to study graphic design at Leeds College of Art. After becoming well known initially for his illustrations which appear on the Gordon Fraser greetings card range, he received critical acclaim for the books which followed, including *Gorilla* and *Willy the Wimp* (Walker Books, 1995).

## WHO'S BEHIND THE DOOR?

### Teaching content

Prediction and repetition are useful structural devices. Illustrations can provide clues for prediction. What characters wear and use as well as what they say and do are important clues for characterisation.

### What you need

*Knock Knock Who's There?*, photocopiable page 88, scissors, scrap paper, writing and drawing materials, character labels (one per child): (1) I'm an alien from outer space (2) I'm an ugly sister (3) I'm a pirate (4) I'm a wicked magic queen.

For the extension activity – photocopiable page 193, chalkboard, writing and drawing materials.

### What to do

Before starting, ensure that children are familiar with stories which have a range of imaginary characters. Show the children the first page of *Knock, Knock Who's There?* Ask them to look carefully at the pattern of the wallpaper around the door and decide which imaginary character will be behind the door. Now ask the children to explain how they knew it would be the gorilla. Ensure that all of the children understand that it was because of the bananas on the wallpaper. If necessary, repeat with a few more pages until you are sure that all of the children understand that an item associated with the character is being used as a clue about who's behind the door. Now go back to the first page. Tell the children to look very carefully at the door. Ask them to explain what there is on the door that gives another clue about who is behind the door. Ensure that all of the children notice the hairy gorilla fingers just above the door handle.

Tell the children that they are going to make their own Knock Knock door and hide an imaginary character behind it. Give the children a copy of photocopiable page 88 (either ready cut out or if the children are able let them cut out the three sides of the door very carefully). Show the children how to fold it in half and let them see how the door works. Give each child one of the character labels. Explain to the children that they are going to draw their own character, and check that they understand who their character is. Tell the children to think about different aspects of their character:

* what the character looks like;
* what he or she does;
* what he or she will be wearing or carrying;
* anything else which the character would use or need.

(If necessary write these prompts on the board.) Remind them to think about their character's hands. What would make them special?

When the children have had a few minutes to think about this, ask each child in turn to describe his or her character, their accessories and their hands (using the prompts if necessary).

When all of the children have had their turn, ask them to draw some small pictures of special things which their character would wear or use, which would give readers a clue about who they were. These might be a crown, a magic mirror, a black magic wand, a space helmet, a flying saucer or clouds, a pirate's hat or eye-patch, a skull and crossbones flag, a pirate ship, a wig, a fan or pointed shoes. Then remind the children that the hand on the door may also give a clue. Give them some scrap paper so that they can practise drawing what their character's hand will look like. The hand they draw might be wearing rings, have long green fingers, or it might be holding something (a sword or a sweet), or wearing gloves (made of lace, leather, wool or gold). Go round and talk to the children about their ideas, giving advice and encouragement. If necessary, the children could refer to some books for ideas about particular characters.

When the children have drawn their ideas, show them the first knock knock picture again. Talk to them about how the pattern is repeated on the wallpaper. Explain to the children that they are going to use some of the drawings they have already tried out to draw their character's border around the sides and the top of the door. Remind them that each item should be drawn so that it is small enough to fit the available space and that it should be repeated regularly around the door. Explain to the children that when they have completed their border pattern they should draw the character's special hand just above the door handle. When all of the front page drawings are finished, the children should draw their character in the space behind the door, remembering to include the details they have used on the front page.

Underneath they should write 'I'm a _____', using their label to help them.

### Further development

When all the drawings have been completed, show the children the second page of the book and remind them what the gorilla said. Tell them that the character said it was going to do something and that this was something a gorilla might do. Look at some of the other characters and discuss what each one said it was going to do. Explain to the children that they are going to decide what their character might say it will do. Give each child a copy of photocopiable page 193 and read over the suggestions. Ask them to choose the statements which they think are most appropriate to their character. Remind them that the statements they choose have to correspond to the actions of their character, for example 'What would a wicked magic queen do?' Let the children cut and paste their chosen suggestion underneath their statement 'I'm a _____'.

Each group's finished knock knock pages can be clipped together to make the children's own version of the knock knock story.

## IF YOU COME IN HERE

### Teaching content
What a character says can show if he or she is brave or frightened.

### What you need
*Knock Knock Who's There?*, photocopiable anthology page 194, and photocopiable pages 195 and 56, scrap paper, glue, writing materials.

### What to do
Show the children a copy of photocopiable anthology page 194 and remind them that each time someone knocked on the door the girl said 'I won't let you in' because she was frightened. Tell the children that this time the girl is going to be brave and is going to say something which will frighten the character away or make it go away for some other reason.

You could model this session by using the characters from the 'Who's Behind the Door?' session. Ask the children for suggestions but also suggest ideas. For example, if the pirate was at the door the little girl might say: 'If you come in here, I'll twang your eye-patch.'

Allocate a character from the book, for example a gorilla, a witch, a ghost, a dragon or a giant, to each pair and give them time to think about and discuss two or three suggestions as to what the girl might say to their character, either to frighten it away or make it go away. Children can note these down on some scrap paper. Go round and offer advice and encouragement. When each pair has some suggestions, ask them to join up with another pair. The first pair should say what their suggestions are and the second pair should

choose the one they think is best for the character and vice versa. When this has been decided, give each pair a speech bubble cut out from a copy of photocopiable page 56 and ask them to write their chosen suggestion in the speech bubble with a felt-tipped pen. When all the speech bubbles are ready, paste them around the copy of photocopiable anthology page 194. Then let the children read what the girl says to chase the characters away. Ask them if they think these are brave things to say and explain why they think so.

To simplify this activity for younger or more inexperienced writers, give each pair a copy of photocopiable page 195. Let them choose from the photocopiable sheet the most appropriate statement which they think the little girl would say to their character. Ask them to cut this out and paste it in the speech bubble.

## FUNNY FEET AND FITTING SHOES

### Teaching content
Characters need to have feet or shoes which are appropriate.

### What you need
*Knock Knock Who's There?*, A5 paper, large sheet of sugar paper, glue, writing and drawing materials.

### What to do
Retell the story, but stop at each page and point out that the character is wearing slippers. Ask the children what each character's feet or shoes should be like. At the end of the story allocate a character to each child (gorilla, witch, ghost, dragon, giant) and ask the children to draw on an A5 sheet some feet or a pair of shoes which would be appropriate for their character.

When all the feet and shoes have been drawn, paste all the drawings of gorilla feet in a row on a large piece of sugar paper. Then underneath these paste a row of witches' shoes and so on. Display the poster in the classroom, either in a writer's area or story corner. Give the children time to look at it later to compare the different illustrations of feet and shoes that were drawn.

to spend a few minutes discussing where their character lives and what that place would look like. They can think about where their character might sit or sleep or eat and about the kinds of things their character would enjoy doing. Go round and talk to them, checking that each pair is thinking of an appropriate place or home for their character. When the children have had time to think and make suggestions, they should draw a home for their creature on to the cartridge paper. Children should take it in turns to draw in details and to suggest ideas. Some children may want to paste on collage materials to provide a textured or patterned effect. When all the drawings have been completed, display them with appropriate headings, explaining who lives in each home.

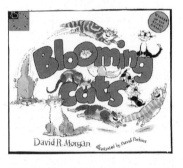

## BLOOMING CATS

*Blooming Cats* by David R. Morgan tells the story of a lonely old man whose chief pleasure is feeding his special friends – the playground cats. One day the old man fails to come and the cats discover he has fallen and is alone in his house. They rescue him by tricking 'a wacky woman' into the house. In hospital the old man makes friends. The book ends with the playground cats, along with the wacky woman and her family, becoming regular visitors to the old man's house.

This book is a good example of a 'happy ending' story. The reader knows that the old man will never be lonely again. It is strong on characterisation, and on using place and setting to create an atmosphere.

Introduce the book by reading the title, author and the dedication. You may like to explain that other children who have heard the story liked it because it is sad, funny, exciting and has a warm, happy ending – the story has something for everyone. Read the story in a way that emphasises how the layout and illustrations contribute to the pace and mood of the story. This is an aspect that is captured very effectively on the story tape and if the

### 4

## WHERE I LIVE

### Teaching content

Characters live in different places. The settings they live in reflect the type of character they are and what they do.

### What you need

Large sheets of cartridge paper, writing and drawing materials, selection of collage materials: cut-up wallpaper, wool, scraps of cloth, shiny paper and so on.

### What to do

Remind the children that each of the characters who knocked on the little girl's door came from a different place. Allocate a character (gorilla, witch, ghost, dragon, giant) to each pair and ask them to think about where that character lives. What kind of place will it be? What kind of house will the character have? What kinds of things will he or she have there? Ask each pair connections between the style of reading and the layout are firmly established on first reading, children will continue to explore and enjoy this when they subsequently listen to the story on tape.

## About the author and illustrator

David Morgan was born in Richmond in Surrey. As well as having written two novels, he is the author of five collections of poetry (including *The Broken Picture Book*), a poetry anthology, and a play *Where's Melissa?* which was screened on ITV. He has been a journalist as well as a writer and spends a great deal of time working with children on creative writing courses.

David Parkins studied wildlife illustration before completing a graphic design course and becoming a freelance illustrator. He has illustrated book covers as well as full-colour picture books, and currently draws the *Desperate Dan* strip in *The Dandy*. David Parkins lives in Lincolnshire with his family and four cats.

### WORDS, PICTURES AND LAYOUT

### Teaching content
Settings created with words and pictures can evoke a particular mood. Layout can make the reader read the story in a particular way.

### What you need
*Blooming Cats*, photocopiable page 196, writing and drawing materials.

### What to do
Read the story to the children or let them listen to the story tape. Ask the children which pages of the story are the most exciting; happy; sad; heart-warming.

Before they decide, briefly review the story, letting them look at the pictures and remember the main events. Then let them look through the book to find one page for each of the above emotions.

They do not all need to agree, but it is important that the children are asked to explain why they have chosen particular pages. The children will probably refer to the following features:

- words used to describe settings and events;
- pictures to show settings.

They will probably not mention the layout of the words and pictures on the page. However, this is also important. Take the opportunity to point out the effect this can have on the way the reader reads the book. For example, during the chase, the words and pictures are all over the page, which makes the reader read it in a disjointed, urgent fashion, whereas when the cats are waiting for the old man, the text is at the top and quite separate from the picture.

Give each child a copy of photocopiable page 196 and ask the children to draw and write down which parts of the story they think best fit the above categories.

### ANOTHER TITLE, ANOTHER STORY

### Teaching content
The title reflects the story; the title is chosen by the author.

### What you need
*Blooming Cats*, marker pens, large strips of paper, display board.

### What to do
Once the children have heard the story and are familiar with the events, ask them to consider the title. Can they suggest why the author chose this title for the book? In what way is it a good title?

The children might mention all sorts of things: it's funny; it reflects what the 'wacky woman' keeps saying; it talks about the main characters, the cats; it makes the reader surprised because they are not really blooming cats at all...

Explain that the author of a book can choose any title he or she wishes. Often, authors write the story and then choose the title, or change it after they have written it – sometimes they don't think of the title until the very end. This may be what David Morgan did. Put the children into pairs and ask them to talk about the book and to decide, if they had written this story, what they would have called it. (Tell them they can't choose *Blooming Cats*.) Once they have

chosen a title, give each pair a marker pen and a strip of paper and ask them to write their title on this.

Display all the titles on the board. Ask the children which ones they like best and why.

### 3

## DEDICATIONS

#### Teaching content

Authors write books, but are also real people, with real families.

#### What you need

*Blooming Cats*, writing materials.

#### What to do

Show the children the dedication page of *Blooming Cats* and point out David Morgan's poem at the top of the page to his daughter Rebecca. Work out how old Rebecca is at present and tell the children.

Ask them how they think she feels, having a dad who has written such a lovely story. What would they feel like? When her friends read the story and enjoy it, what will she say to them? Will she tell them it was written by her dad? What would her friends say? Will they believe her?

This is a wonderful story and the children

will agree that it would be lovely to have such a book dedicated to them. However, *they* also write wonderful stories. Ask the children to whom they would like to dedicate a story – it has to be someone really special. Ask them to think of the best story which they have written recently and to write a short piece (it doesn't need to be a poem) dedicating this to a special person in their lives.

### 4

## FIRST AND LAST

#### Teaching content

What makes a satisfying ending? The detail in pictures can help create particular reactions and feelings in the reader.

#### What you need

*Blooming Cats*, photocopiable anthology page 197, chalkboard, drawing materials.

#### What to do

Read the children *Blooming Cats*, or remind them of the story. Ask them to look at the picture on the first page of the story (page 5). What does this picture tell them about the old man and his life? Ask them to suggest words to capture some of their feelings or reactions. They may suggest cosy, quiet, boring, lonely, shy, sad, peaceful, comfortable and so on. Write these words on the board.

Then ask the children to look at the last picture in the book. Point out that it is a scene in the same room and that the old man is doing exactly the same thing – drinking a cup of tea. However, this picture has quite a different feel to it. What words could they suggest to describe this picture? They might suggest cheerful, busy, noisy, bustling, popular, exciting, happy. Write these words on the board also.

Point out that this picture makes a good ending because it is so hopeful. The reader knows that the old man is not going to be lonely in his house any more as his friends will come to visit him regularly.

Now give each child a copy of photocopiable anthology page 197 (enlarged if necessary). Explain that this page is a copy of the picture on page 6. Tell the children to look at the page carefully. Which word list on the board best applies to this picture? Ask the children what details they could add to the picture to make it give rise to feelings more like those in the final list and picture. They may suggest children playing, people shopping, cars, animals and so on. Ask each child to add details to the picture which would make it happier.

**Teaching content**
Different characters do and say different things.

**What you need**
*Blooming Cats*, photocopiable page 198, scissors, glue, paper.

**What to do**
Remind the children of the different characters by rereading the pages which name and describe the ten playground cats. Introduce photocopiable page 198 which has four cats pictured at the top. Give each child a copy of the sheet and explain that these cats have found a parcel in the street. Each cat reacts differently to it, and what they say is in the speech bubbles on the sheet.

Tell the children to cut out the cats and stick them on to a sheet of paper, leaving plenty of

space between each one. Then ask them to cut out the speech bubbles and match each speech bubble to the appropriate cat, pasting the speech bubble in the right place. Finally, let the children colour in the pictures.

## A SCARY STORY

*A Scary Story*, written and illustrated by Peter Bailey, tells a simple story about two cats, Tina and Tom, who are going to look for the 'Ghost of Grim Grange'. Having collected what they need, they set off with a knapsack and torch to find the building. Through a creaky door and up creaky stairs, the cats make their journey until they find a door, which has a sign saying 'DO NOT COME IN, GHOST'. After some indecision, they open the door. The ghost is immediately revealed, and in contrast to the slow pace of the first part of the book, there is the urgency of the race for home after the ghost's appearance. This is created by the short exclamations as the cats run away terrified. The cats finally reach home, and on the final page they have already rewritten the story of what happened: 'I think we were quite brave...', they said.

Within the book, there are opportunities for developing children's awareness of characterisation, structure and place. The expressions on the cats' faces: confidence at the start; hesitation inside the Grange; mixed emotions outside the ghost's door; and terror on the return journey, all offer good opportunities for young children to empathise with the characters.

The setting is scary – the torchlight features heavily in the story, helping Tina and Tom to find their way in the dark outside their house, then to identify Grim Grange, lighting their way in the hallway and along the corridors, and allowing them to focus on the writing on the door. It is interesting to note that although the cats rely on their torch very much at the beginning of the story, it is dropped at the sight of the ghost and the cats manage to get home without it.

A picture of the two cats at home with their soup and sandwiches, sitting in armchairs in front of the fire, reveals a calmness to the final page. Young children will easily identify with this kind of ending. You could ask them: Do you think they were brave? Did you think they would get caught? Do you think they will ever go back there again? Would you?

## About the author and illustrator

Peter Bailey was born in India where his father worked on the railways. When his family returned to London, his father got a job at the Victoria and Albert Museum where Peter first became interested in art. He has worked as an illustrator since 1969. His latest book, which he has illustrated for Scholastic Children's Books, is *Dolphinella*; he has also illustrated *Tigerella*.

## MY OWN SCARY STORY

### Teaching content

The front cover of a story book can tell the reader what type of story it is.

### What you need

*A Scary Story*, chalkboard, writing and drawing materials.

### What to do

Show the children the front cover of the book *A Scary Story* and ask them to tell you all the things which they think make this a scary story. List or draw these on the board.

When the children make suggestions, ask them what the mice, cats and ghost look like, and add their descriptive words to the list. Now

ask the children to think of any other scary stories they may have read.
- Where did these take place?
- Who was in the story?
- What made it scary?

Add the children's suggestions to the original list, perhaps in a different-coloured pen. Tell the children that they are going to design the front cover of a scary book, and for a few minutes you would like them to think about what they are going to draw. Ask them to close their eyes. When their eyes are closed, go over some of the ideas mentioned in the class brainstorm.

Ask the children to write down some of the things which they would put on their own front cover. Let them use some of the words on the board. You may have to scribe or provide words. Some children may like to make a brief drawing as a draft.

Now ask the children to draw their picture on a separate sheet of paper. This would be effective as a black-line drawing with felt-tipped pen. It could be coloured later to add effect. They can give their picture a heading 'A Scary Story'.

When all the drawings have been completed, ask the children to show their picture to the person next to them and tell him or her why their story is scary.

These covers could be used in three ways: as a class display on the wall; for children's stories to be written as a follow-up; or for a collated class book of scary covers for books.

## EYES EVERYWHERE!

### Teaching content

The expression on a character's face tells you how he or she is feeling.

### What you need

*A Scary Story*, photocopiable page 199, chalkboard, Blu-Tack, glue.
For the extension activity – paper plates for masks.

### What to do

Gather the children together, ensuring that they are all able to see the pictures in the book.

Tell the children that you want them to look at the pictures of the cats, paying particular attention to the eyes and the mouth in each one, to see how they look and feel in different parts of the story. Draw their attention to the pictures of Tina and Tom:

- standing side by side on page 4;
- looking around 'along the gloomy corridor...';
- pointing to the 'ghost' sign with the torch;
- seeing the ghost and running away;
- safe in their house.
  At each point discuss:
- How do you think the cat is feeling?
- What tells you that in the way in which the face has been drawn?

Make a list of the words offered to you on a large piece of paper. These should include happy, not sure, looking around, angry, and frightened.

Finally, ask the children if they can make a face which expresses these various emotions. Let them work in pairs to do this and to note how faces can show a full range of expressions.

Give each child a copy of photocopiable page 199 and remind the children of some of the expressions and feelings which you have talked about. You may have to read aloud some of the words at the foot of the page for the children. Explain that you would like them to cut out the words and paste each word under the most suitable picture. It may help if they use Blu-Tack first, then paste them on to the sheet after you have checked their work and discussed it. Finally, let the children devise one of their own expressions for the last cat picture and then write a word(s) to describe how the cat looks and feels.

## Further development

An appropriate follow-up to this activity would be to provide masks for the children which have different expressions. Simple paper-plate masks would be suitable. Using these, children could develop conversations based on the mood of the characters in the story.

### IF I MET THE SCARY GHOST...

## Teaching content

Different characters can react in different ways.

## What you need

Photocopiable page 200, writing and drawing materials, three pieces of card, each one with a different word or phrase: (1) The Ghost! (2) Help! (3) Run! Run! Run!

## What to do

Gather the class together and remind the children of the part of the story where the two cats met the ghost. The ghost said 'Whoooooooo!', Tina and Tom ran, shouting 'Help!' Ask the children to think for a minute about what they might say if they were in the story and had met the ghost too. Now ask them to tell the person sitting next to them what they would say, and then to listen while their partner repeats the procedure.

Ask selected children to tell the whole class what their partners said they would say.

Compare some of the suggestions given by the children.

Remind the children that in the story the cats ran away quickly. Ask the children if they would do the same or would they do something else: for example, stand very still; wave their hands in the air; jump up and down; tiptoe quickly away; step back and keep walking backwards.

Show the children photocopiable page 200 and explain what you would like them to do. They should first of all draw a picture of themselves in the space provided, adding as much detail as possible to their face, and making sure that they draw their arms appropriately.

Stop and explore this for a moment with the children, and use one of the examples previously given by them: for example, if a child said he or she would say 'Go away!' ask this child to stand up and say it. Tell the others to look at his or her face and notice any movement as the child speaks. Does the child's face look angry? Is the child pointing, with his or her arm outstretched? Encourage the children to think about this as they draw the picture of themselves.

Then tell them to write what they would say in the speech bubble. Ask the children to consider how this will be written. Draw their attention to the cards you have made, showing how words may be written in big letters, bold letters, with the same word repeated, with an exclamation mark afterwards and so on.

For the third part of the sheet, ask the children to either draw a picture of or write about what they would do next.

The children's contributions should be shared with the whole class when they have completed their photocopiable sheets.

## IF I WAS THE SCARY GHOST...

**Teaching content**

Stories can be told from different viewpoints.

**What you need**

Writing materials (if required).

**What to do**

As in the previous activity, remind the children of the part of the story where the two cats met the ghost. Ask the children to think for a minute about what they might say (and think) if they were the ghost in the story. What would they think if someone came into their bedroom? Why might they chase after Tom and Tina? Put the children into pairs and ask them to tell the story from the ghost's viewpoint. If appropriate, ask the children to write this story.

## IN THE TORCHLIGHT

**Teaching content**

The use of detail can create atmosphere. An item like a torch in a story can add effect by focusing on this.

**What you need**

*A Scary Story*, photocopiable page 201, display board, sheet of A3 paper, drawing materials, four pieces of card, each one with a different phrase: (1) name on the gate (2) behind the door (3) up the stairs (4) on the sign.

**What to do**

As you look through the story with the children, ask them about what the characters might see in the beam of the torch. Before you turn each relevant page ask:

- what might be in the garden (plants, garden furniture, statues, animals);
- what might be in the hallway;
- what might be up the stairs.

Tell the children that for this activity they are going to work in pairs, pretending that they are Tina and Tom in another scary place. They will have to discuss and decide on:
- a name for their scary place;
- the scary things they might see
  - behind the door;
  - up the stairs;
  - on the sign.

Attach the cards you have made to a display board and let the children discuss these points in their pairs. Give each pair a copy of photocopiable page 201 and explain that you would like the children to draw the scary things which the torch is showing in each picture.

Finally, bring the whole class back together and on a large piece of paper record the children's ideas, using the words on the cards as four headings. As a class, ask the children to tell you which suggestions they like best and why.

## SAFE AT LAST?

### Teaching content
Stories can have different turning points and endings.

### What you need
*A Scary Story*, photocopiable page 202, large sheet of paper, scissors, Blu-Tack, writing and drawing materials.

### What to do
Gather the children together as a class and show them the final part of the story when the two cats run out of 'Grim Grange'. Ask the children to close their eyes and think about what might have happened if Tina and Tom had got to the gates, but the gates had been locked.

Take suggestions from the children as to what might have happened next and record these on a large sheet of paper under the heading 'Gates locked'. Some children may come up with one action; for example, 'The cats climbed the gates.' Encourage the children

to think through what happened after that and then give further suggestions, such as 'ran home'. Now encourage the children to think about other things which could have happened and how these could have changed the ending to the story. For example:
- They meet a friend.
- Tom drops the knapsack.
- They get lost in the house.
- The ghost is friendly.

When you have received enough ideas to provide a stimulus for this activity, explain to the children that you would like them to draw what happened, thereby presenting an alternative ending to the story about Tina and Tom, and to write about it. Emphasise that the ending will be different from the one in the book. Give each child a copy of photocopiable page 202. Tell the children to draw their picture in the box on the photocopiable sheet and write their text underneath it. You may have to scribe for some children. When they have finished, cut off the stories on the bottom part of the sheet and display the various endings on large pieces of paper on the wall.

Read these to the whole class and let the children talk about which ending they liked best and why.

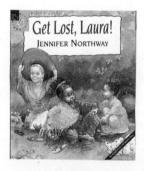

## GET LOST, LAURA!

*Get Lost, Laura!* by Jennifer Northway tells a realistic story and has three central characters: Lucy, her baby sister Laura and her cousin Alice. The two older girls wish that Laura would 'get lost'. She spoils their play by taking the high-heeled shoes from Lucy as she dresses up, and then another pair of shoes and a hat. Eventually, they tire of this and decide to hide, knowing that Mum had told them to watch and play with Laura. When they come out of the shed, their hiding place, to find Laura, they realise that she is missing. They try to find her, Lucy feels herself starting to panic and an argument ensues between the two girls, each girl accusing the other. This is followed by tears and Lucy's resignation that she will have to tell Mum, but when the girls go to the kitchen they find Laura sitting on Mum's knee. There is a sense of relief, and this time, when Laura is about to take something from Lucy, she is not so inclined to say 'Get Lost, Laura'.

The story has a real-life family situation with which many children may empathise, particularly if they have a younger brother or sister, or even if they are the youngest and have experienced this reaction to them before. The children in the story show real emotion, which is depicted both in the story-line and in the facial expressions: annoyance at Laura; curiosity in the shed; disgust when looking under the cabbages and in the dustbins; panic as they look for Laura in vain, anger when arguing with each other, upset as they become overwhelmed by the situation; then surprise at seeing Laura in the kitchen and relief at finding her safe.

The story takes place in different settings, the illustrations containing plenty of detail for discussion. It is structured to show maximum pace at the crisis point of not finding Laura, with resultant feelings of fear and worry maintaining the pace of the story towards the resolution at the end.

## About the author and illustrator

Jennifer Northway's career in children's books began as an illustrator. It was with her *Lucy* stories for Scholastic Children's books that she began to write as well as to illustrate. Jennifer Northway was brought up in Africa and South America and after her marriage lived in St. Lucia. She now lives in Rome with her husband and young daughter.

**1**

## OUR STORY ABOUT LAURA

### Teaching content

Through children's own imaginative play, stories can be reviewed, changed and created using an initial stimulus of the text.

### What you need

*Get Lost, Laura!*, an area where children can act out the story, box with dressing-up clothes similar to the story, six character cards, each identifying a different character name (tied with ribbon so that the children can wear them), writing materials.

### What to do

Begin by reading the whole book again to the class. When you have finished, ask the children some key questions about the story.
• Did you think that Lucy and Alice were right to run away and hide?
• What would you do?
• Where would you hide from Laura?
• What might happen to Laura?
• What would you do next?
• What kind of ending would your story have?

Put the children into groups of six. Show the children the box of clothes and explain to them that in the area set aside, for example the home corner, they can act out the story or make up their own story about Laura. Each of the main characters should wear a character name card. Make time to remind the children of some of the actions in the story, the ways the characters felt and how they showed this. Leave the book with the children so that they may look at it to plan their play, or go back to it, either for ideas or to reflect at the end. Three other children may play and could take on the role of Mum and the neighbours or could be other characters as the children choose.

At a feedback session, ask the children to tell the others about the story they created. Let the children take the lead in relating what they did, but prompt where necessary with questions which will enable them to talk about the characters they became, their feelings, actions and why they chose the ending to their 'story'.

Finally, ask each child to draw a picture of what they did, or at least their favourite part of it. In their groups of six, the children could each draw a different part of the story, which could then be collated to form a book for the class. Try to encourage children to use dialogue in their text by asking them 'What did you say then?' and so on. For younger children, a single picture may suffice, with you scribing the story.

These pictures could be displayed around the imaginative area in which children are using *Get Lost, Laura!* as a stimulus for their own story-making.

### WHEN I WAS LITTLE

#### Teaching content
Characters can be shown through appearance, action and speech.

#### What you need
*Get Lost, Laura!*, a picture of each child when he or she was little (between the ages of 18 months and three years old would be ideal), photocopiable page 203, Blu-Tack, chalkboard, writing and drawing materials.

#### What to do
In advance of this activity, children need to bring to school a picture of themselves when they were younger, about the same age as Laura is in the story.

Read *Get Lost, Laura!* to the children or listen to it together on the story tape. Ask the children how old they think Laura is and why. The children will probably mention:
• things Laura does (cries, wants to join in, pulls things, wanders off);
• things Laura says ('I want them');
• what Laura looks like (too small for the clothes, wobbly on high-heeled shoes and so on);
• what other characters say about Laura.

Then ask individual children to show their photographs to the class and tell the other children what they:
• looked like when they were little like Laura;
• liked to play with;
• talked about, and how they talked;
• what others said about them.

As they do this, list key words offered by the children under the headings 'looked like', 'played with', 'talked about'. Write the children's suggestions on the board.

Give out copies of photocopiable page 203 and explain that, first of all, you would like each child to place his or her photograph in the box on the sheet under the words 'I looked like' and then attach the photograph with Blu-Tack. Under the words 'but look at me now' the children should draw a picture of how they look today. Ask them to write three words or more about what they looked like then and about what they look like now under the boxes.

Explain to the children that they may fill in the next sections on the sheet, writing about what they played with in the past and what they play with now, and similarly for things they used to say, compared with what they like to talk about now.

At a feedback session, provide an opportunity for the children to show their drawings to others or in small groups to read what they have written.

### LOST! STORIES OF THE SEARCH

#### Teaching content
Stories take place in different settings.

#### What you need
*Get Lost, Laura!*, small pieces of card or paper (each one with the word 'found' on it), glue, writing and drawing materials.

#### What to do
Gather the children together and remind them of the places in which Lucy and Alice looked for Laura.
• in the shed (and under it);
• in the suitcase;
• in the cabbages;
• in the dustbin;

- in the field;
- next-door's flowerbed.

Ask the children to think of other places, perhaps in the house, where Laura could have hidden. List the children's suggestions on a large sheet of paper.

Tell the children that they are going to draw different places where Laura may have hidden, and one place where she might be found. Give each child a sheet of A4 paper and ask the children to draw three places where Laura could hide and one place where she could be found. Then ask them to write a description of the places underneath each picture they have drawn. (You could help the children with the layout of the sheet by giving them A4 paper on which you have drawn boxes for them to draw their pictures in.) Tell the children to stick their 'found' labels above the appropriate picture.

Finally, the children should read their story of Laura's hiding places to others, comparing the different places that they have chosen.

## I DON'T LIKE IT WHEN OTHERS TELL ME...

### Teaching content
Characters in stories have feelings. What people say and how they speak can portray and create emotions.

### What you need
*Get Lost, Laura!*, photocopiable page 204, writing and drawing materials.

### What to do
Show the children the book *Get Lost, Laura!*, focusing their attention on the first part of the story. Ask the children to tell you all of the things that Alice and Lucy said to Laura:
- 'Oh, push off...'
- 'Why don't you go and play in the sandpit?'
- 'Get lost...'
- 'Go away.'

Ask the children if anyone has ever said anything like that to them. Explore with the whole class times when they have not liked how others have spoken to them, or times when they have not liked being told what to do. Ask them the following questions:
- Who says it?

- Why do they say it?
- How do they say it?
- How do you feel?
- What do you do or say?

For example, has Mum ever said 'Go and play with your toys' in a loud voice because she is busy? Ask the children if they felt angry and stamped their feet, or if they felt sad and cried. Spend some time on this until you have discussed enough instances with the children to enable most to join in.

Give each child a copy of photocopiable page 204 and tell the children that now you want each of them to draw and write about a time when others have told them to do something because they were displeased with them. Tell the children to draw a picture of the person who spoke to them under the words 'Who says it?' Ask them to write in the speech bubble what that person said. Then they should write why they thought that person said what they did. In the box they should draw a picture of themselves and write next to it about how they felt when the person spoke to them in this particular way.

## THE GARDEN

The magical text and atmospheric illustrations of *The Garden* by Dyan Sheldon and Gary Blythe evoke a setting for a story which is haunting and imaginative. A young girl finds a strange stone in her garden. Her mother's explanation that it might have been there for hundreds of years calls up a dream or a memory of long ago, and of the people who inhabited this place in the past.

This book will be suitable for the older and more experienced writers in this age group. They will appreciate both the imaginative, dream-like quality of the illustrations and the beautifully crafted text which describes the atmosphere and settings perfectly. Read the story to small groups of children so that from the beginning they can enjoy the illustrations which enrich the story. Give children time to re-examine and mull over the illustrations and the text on their own. The story tape can provide valuable support to these reflective activities.

### About the author and illustrator

Dyan Sheldon was born and educated in New York. Equally successful as an adult and children's writer, her children's book *The Whales' Song* (Century Hutchinson) – illustrated by Gary Blythe – won the 1990 Kate Greenaway Medal. She is the author of the highly successful *Harry and Chicken* series and a young adult fiction book *Tall, Thin and Blonde* (both published by Walker Books), the latter having featured on *The Sunday Times* Bestseller List. Dyan Sheldon divides her time between New York and her home in north London.

Gary Blythe was born in Liverpool. He specialised in illustration on a graphic design course which he studied at Liverpool Polytechnic before moving to London to work. He is married and now lives in Merseyside. When he is not working he enjoys photography and walking in the countryside.

## SHE HAD NEVER SEEN ANYTHING QUITE LIKE IT BEFORE...

### Teaching content
Detail of setting and description. Selecting a few well-chosen words for a concise but vivid description.

### What you need
A collection of interesting and varied stones, a basket to present them in, chalkboard, writing and drawing materials.

### What to do
Show the children the first illustration in the book and read them the description:

> Jenny found a stone while she was digging in the garden. It was dark and rough and came to a point. She had never seen anything quite like it before.

Next, ask each child to choose a stone from the basket. Let them have time to look at it, touch it and think about how they would describe this stone. Then ask each child to describe his or her stone using a few well-chosen words. When everyone has had a turn, ask the children to think for a minute about where their chosen stone might have been found. Discuss the children's suggestions and note these on the board. Again, encourage the children to use a few words which are appropriate and, as you note them down, suggest ways in which their words could be expanded into an evocative description. For example, if a child says his or her stone was found in a stream, you could suggest: 'in a slowly, flowing stream at the bottom of a deep dark pool, among the autumn leaves'.

Explain to the children that you would like them to write a short description of their stone and where it was found, in a style of writing which is similar to the one in the book. Explain that they should substitute their own name for the name 'Jenny', and describe where the stone was found and exactly what it was like. Give the children an outline of this on the board.

_____ found the stone ... It was ...

Explain that when they have finished they should draw their stone and where it was found, using the illustration in the book to give them ideas on style. Remind them to choose suitable colours and to start with the background of where the stone was found. Tell them that the surrounding details of the setting can be slightly smudged if they wish, but the stone should be drawn clearly against the background.

The completed drawings and writing should be pasted side by side on white backing paper. Suggest that the children use a ruler to draw two fine black lines to make a border around two edges of their writing, as in the book. The finished work can then be displayed above a table, on which you have placed the book (open at the relevant page).

## FROM THE CENTRE TO THE EDGE

### Teaching content
Using viewpoint to structure a description.

### What you need
Access to a suitable outdoor area, clipboards, writing materials.

### What to do
Read the children the second page of the story before they go outside, or, if it is a fine day, gather the children together outside and read the page to them there. Focus on the description of the garden and examine with the children the way in which the garden is described and how it spreads out from a given point. Ask the children to choose a central point in their outdoor area and to describe what is there. Next, ask them to imagine a circle drawn around this point, a little way out. What do they see along the circumference of the circle? How would they describe it? Now ask them to imagine a circle at the furthest edge of the school grounds (or the outdoor area in which this activity is taking place). Tell the children to work in pairs and write a short description of what they can see. Still thinking of their imaginary circles, they should describe in one sentence what is in the centre and then a sentence to describe the circle which is further out and then finally describe what is in the furthest circle, far away in the distance. Remind the children that a few well-chosen words are better than a long

complicated description. Give each pair time to think about and note down their ideas. Then ask each pair to write their descriptions clearly on paper.

Back in the classroom, mount the descriptions around a circular piece of paper and display in the writer's area.

## NIGHT SKY/MORNING SKY

### Teaching content
Careful selection of descriptive words can evoke the mood and physical detail of the setting.

### What you need
*The Garden*, scrap paper, A4 white card, writing materials.

### What to do
Read the children the section in the book which describes the dream Jenny had of the Indian encampment, or let them listen to this section of the tape. Focus on the description: 'The moon was corn-yellow and the stars sat low in a blue-black sky.'

Tell the children to close their eyes and to try to imagine what Jenny saw. What do they think the sky looked like at night? Discuss with them the short but descriptive way the writer has painted a mind-picture of the sky. Identify the few aspects described: the moon, the stars and the sky. Ask the children how the author has described these and try to elicit from them that the author has used colour words to describe them. The description of the position of the stars is also important.

Show them the illustration which accompanies the text. Explore with them how well this matches their own mental image. Explain to the children that they too are going to write a short description which will create a mind-picture for the reader. Show them the morning page at the end of the book and ask them to look closely at the illustration of the sky. Explain that this is the time of day called 'dawn' or 'first light'. Tell the children that they are going to create a mind-picture of this sky at dawn, using a few descriptive words. Ask the children what aspects of the sky they think are important to describe. What colours will they select and how will they describe them? Will the

position of any aspect be significant?

Put the children into pairs and tell them to discuss these points with each other and try out various phrases to describe the sky in the morning. When they are satisfied, they should write their final description in fairly large black print on A4 card and draw a fine-lined black border around their writing.

Place the cards in a box beside *The Garden* on the table in the book area. At story time, or any other suitable time, pairs of children should be encouraged to open the book at the morning page and look at the illustration. Then they should select two or three descriptions and read these. They should decide which one they think is best and prop it up by the open book. Other pairs can take it in turns to do the same.

## A DREAM

### Teaching content

People build up different mind-pictures of scenes and settings in stories.

### What you need

Drawing materials.

### What to do

Give the children some A4 drawing paper and coloured chalks and pastels. Tell them that they are going to draw a scene from the story of *The Garden*. Explain to the children that you are going to read a section of the book to them which describes the scene, or you could listen to this section on the tape together. Remind them of the hazy subdued colours used in the illustrations and that these should be used when they draw the scene. Ask them to close their eyes while you read, and to try to imagine the scene which Jenny saw.

Read the children the section in the book which describes the dream Jenny had of the Indian encampment. It starts with the description used in the 'Night sky/morning sky' activity: 'The moon was corn-yellow and the stars sat low in a blue-black sky.'

Without talking about the description, ask the children to draw the scene of the Indian camp as they imagined it looked to Jenny. When the children have completed their drawings, put them into pairs. Each pair should show their drawings to each other, explaining them and then comparing them. They should pay particular attention to the differences between their drawings.

The completed drawings should be mounted on dark paper and displayed in the corridor, so that the children can look at them over a period of time and identify all the different mind-pictures the description conveys. The excerpt from the book should be displayed beside the drawings.

## THE ORIGINAL AMERICAN PEOPLE

### Teaching content

Description of setting provides information about characters and their lives. Visualising characters in their setting accentuates these characters.

### What you need

Writing materials.

### What to do

Tell the children that the story they have been reading was set in America. The people who are referred to in the book as 'Indians' were the people who lived in North America before settlers moved in from Britain and Europe. This story provides lots of detail about what these people were like and how they lived their lives. Explain to the children that you are going to read the part of the story where Jenny dreams about the Indian camp and the people who lived there, or listen to this on the tape. Tell the children that they must imagine that they were with Jenny in her tent and that they saw what she saw and did what she did. Ask the children to imagine the people who Jenny might have seen or met as she walked through the camp. Tell the children to close their eyes and rest their heads on the table, or their arms if they find this more comfortable.

Read the story, starting from: 'The moon was corn-yellow and the stars sat low...' and continue to '...and time was measured by the changings of the moon'.

When you have finished reading, ask the children to think about one person they imagined in the story. It might be one of the men sitting round the camp-fire, or a woman sitting at the door of her tepee or a child sleeping inside the tent. Tell the children that they are going to draw a picture of that person but before they draw they must think about:

• what the person looks like;
• what kind of hairstyle he or she has;
• what he or she wears (clothes, shoes and jewellery);
• how the person spends his or her time;
• what kinds of things he or she does for work and for play;
• what the person likes to do at the end of the day;
• what kind of stories the person likes to hear.

The amount of discussion of these points will depend on the previous experience of the children and how much prompting they need.

When the children have completed their drawings, tell them that they must think about and identify the most important things about this person and how they would describe the person to another child. Remind the children to describe only a few significant features, using several well-chosen words. The children may make brief notes or labels and attach these at appropriate points on their drawing. For some children this may be a sufficiently challenging task.

Others might be encouraged to use these notes to select significant features and a few appropriate phrases in order to write a short description of this person. Remind the children that this should help the reader to create a vivid mind-picture of the person.

The drawings can be displayed on the other side of the corridor from the camp drawings, with the children's labels in place, or with their descriptive writing underneath the picture.

## THE HOUSE CAT

*The House Cat* by Helen Cooper tells the story of Tom-Cat who lives in a house with two families; he is the House Cat. At the beginning of the story the two households are described, and it is immediately apparent that the two abodes within the house – upstairs and downstairs – provide settings for the House Cat which are very different from each other. Life with Jennifer means warmth and comfort; with the Spode-Fawcetts things are much colder – in their home Tom-Cat's main task is to 'match the carpet'.

One day the Spode-Fawcetts move. The House Cat is put into a cardboard box and has to rely on his senses to pick up knowledge about his journey. He smells 'something good', sees birds, hears the noises of traffic, senses dogs.

Unhappy in his new environment, and unwanted by the Spode-Fawcetts, he sets off for home, remembering what he saw, heard, sensed and smelled on his journey. Tom-Cat avoids dogs, cars and swans (and narrowly misses being a 'Boat-Cat') to arrive home safely. A new family has moved in downstairs and Tom-Cat reasserts his position as the House Cat.

Tom-Cat is a strong central character who will appeal to young children as they become involved in his struggles. That he belongs to himself and no one else is demonstrated by his stubborn refusal to be owned by a single household and is emphasised by the repetition of the phrase 'I am the House Cat'.

The characters of Jennifer and the Spode-Fawcetts are drawn with skilful use of actions, environments, speech and appearance.

Layout and illustration do much to set the mood and pace of the story. When Tom-Cat is placed in the boot of a car, the pages have a black background and white text, symbolising the darkness of the box and the darkness of this episode in Tom-Cat's life. His restricted and episodic glimpses of the journey, through the hole in the box, are represented by a series of small pictures, in strong contrast to the continuous, impressionistic reconstruction in his head, which is almost dream-like.

The return journey is described with short, repetitive phrases, creating excitement and pace. An important feature of the book is the varying size of the illustrations and the way that the page is divided, each illustration pinpointing a different focus of the House Cat's journey.

You will find that it is easy to read the story to children in a way that underlines many of these points. Simply by pausing, altering the tone and volume of the voice, and pointing to pictures as you read, the children can be encouraged to make good use of pictures, layout and language when they listen to the story on tape at a later date.

## About the author and illustrator

Helen Cooper trained as a music teacher. She wrote and illustrated her first children's picture book *Kit and the Magic Kite* in 1986, while by day she painted ceramic figurines. Her glowing colours and exquisite detail have been her hallmark and her work has been exhibited in London and New York. She has illustrated several children's books, some of which she has written herself. *Bear Under the Stairs* was shortlisted for the Smarties Prize.

**THE WAY HOME**

## Teaching content

Short, direct phrases can be used to increase the pace of the story. Longer, descriptive phrases slow the pace and give the story a more leisurely feel.

### What you need

*The House Cat*, photocopiable page 205, scissors, glue, writing materials.

### What to do

Read the children the part of the story where the cat is running home ('He must go quickly, no time for play' up to 'He knows that smell!'), or let them listen to this section on the tape, but do not let them look at the pictures in the book.

Ask the children where they think the cat was running during the journey. How do they know this? They will probably talk about their memories of hearing the story before – understandings gleaned from the pictures and particular events such as the reasons for the cat stopping (the river, the boat). Ask the children to close their eyes and listen to the words as you read them again.

Ask them if there is anything about the language that makes the first part of the journey seem to pass quickly. The children will probably talk about the way you read the story – the tone of voice, volume, speed and urgency in the reading. Show the children the text and explain that you read it in this way because of the way it has been written. When the cat is running, the words and phrases are short and repetitive. When the cat is still, or moving slowly, the phrases are longer, more continuous and descriptive.

Show the children a copy of photocopiable page 205 and explain that the pictures describe a journey home from school. Talk through the route: out of the school gates, past the shops, past the play park and up the garden path to home. Point to each of the pictures as you do this.

Put the children into pairs. Explain that the children are going to describe a journey of a child *running* home or a child *strolling* home. Show them how to cut out the four pictures and stick them on to a blank sheet of paper, leaving a space underneath each one for the text. Tell them not to tell any other pair which kind of journey they have chosen.

Now draw the children's attention to the phrases and sentences on the photocopiable sheet and read them through. Explain that some of the phrases on the sheet are long, continuous and descriptive, and some are short and urgent. Ask each pair to construct a description of a journey home by selecting appropriate phrases from the sheet to describe either a child running home or a child strolling home. Tell the children to cut out the boxes of text and paste them below the appropriate pictures. Before the children begin work, remind them once again of the cat's journey home and of how the language showed when the cat was running, or moving slowly.

When the children have finished, ask each pair to read their description to the class. Can the children guess whether this was a description of the settings as seen by someone travelling quickly or someone travelling slowly?

## Teaching content
Attention to detail in describing settings; one strategy for structuring description.

### What you need
*The House Cat*, squares of card, card with a 'viewing window' hole (approximately 8cm × 8cm) cut out from the middle of each square, writing and drawing materials.

### What to do
Show the children the pages of *The House Cat* in which the cat is looking through a hole in the box at the scenes he passes on his journey to the new house. Explain that this is one way to get an original description of a new place, or journey, and the restricted vision makes you notice things that you would normally overlook.

Give the children the squares of card with the 'viewing window' holes cut out. Show them how they can use these to 'frame' small areas of the classroom. Explain how the 'frame' narrows in focus when it is held slightly away from the eye. Let them experiment for a few minutes and then ask volunteers to describe the detail of one 'frame' which they have seen through their card. Can the other children guess which part of the classroom is being described? (The children could use their viewing windows throughout the school, if you think this is appropriate.) Tell the children to listen carefully so that they understand what they have to do.

Ask the children to use their viewing windows to select *one* frame from the classroom. They must look carefully through their 'window' and draw *exactly* what they see. Emphasise that the detail in the drawing is very important. When the children have done a detailed drawing, ask

them to write a few sentences to describe the drawing. You may wish to suggest that they move away from describing physical objects and, like Tom-Cat, describe the objects in terms of their own thoughts, senses or reactions (describing how they can smell... see... hear... touch... sense... know...).

When the children have finished, encourage them to share their drawings and writings with the rest of the class, and to let other children guess which part of the classroom or school the 'frame' is from. Use the drawings and writing to make a wall display or class book. If placed in sequence, they can form an effective and unusual description of a journey through the classroom, or around the school.

## Teaching content
Description of setting reflects the person who describes it. Different characters notice different things.

### What you need
*The House Cat*, drawing materials.

### What to do
With the children gathered together, look at the page in *The House Cat* when Tom-Cat recalls everything he saw and sensed on his journey in the cardboard box. Read the text on the page to the children '... and somehow, in his head he knows the way'. Show the children the picture, and talk to them about what Tom-Cat is remembering.

Ask the children:
• What kinds of things is Tom-Cat thinking of?
• Why were these important things for Tom-Cat to remember?

Now tell the children that they are going to think about finding their way home. What would help them to remember the journey home?

Tell the children to close their eyes and think of their journey home from school. Tell them to think of special places, animals or people they always see at different points of the journey and why they remember them. Talk them through

all the things they may have seen or heard.
- Do you cross a road? Is it busy? Can you hear the noise of the cars or buses?
- Are there animals you want to meet or want to avoid?
- Do you pass by a park, bus stop, shops? Are there special smells or noises or other sensations you associate with them?
- Do you see any signs? What do they say?
- Is there a special place?
  - railings or a hedge you trail you finger on?
  - a wall you walk along or jump over?
  - a house with a high hedge?

When you have given sufficient prompting, tell the children to open their eyes and try to draw on a sheet of A4 paper as many things as they can remember about their journey home – the kinds of things that would help them if they were lost and had to get home like Tom-Cat.

When they have finished, pair the children to 'tell' their story about the type of things which would help them find their way back home.

### Further development

This activity may be extended with older children or more experienced writers by asking them to annotate the individual drawings on their page with phrases or words which convey why they are significant, and what makes the places or features memorable to them. Remind the children that, like Tom-Cat, this might be a special smell or something worrying. For example:
- the smell from the bakery;
- the barking dogs;
- the tingle from trailing fingers on the railings.

The drawings and writing can be displayed, or collated to make a book of 'Journeys home'.

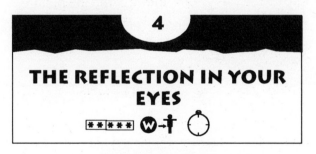

## THE REFLECTION IN YOUR EYES

### Teaching content
Characterisation through the choices individuals make.

### What you need
*The House Cat*, oval-shaped black paper, white eye-shapes, glue, chalk, drawing materials.

### What to do
Read the first few pages of the story, up to 'But what's all this?' Ask the children what sort of cat they think Tom-Cat is. For example, does he care what people think of him? Why does he visit Jennifer? Why does he visit the Spode-Fawcetts? Does he see himself as a guest? Does he see himself as a pet? Who does he think owns the house? Does he need people, or think that people need him?

Ask the children to look at the illustration of the cat's eyes on page 5. Why do they think it is important that the whole house is reflected in his eyes? What does this tell them about Tom-Cat and about what he thinks is important?

Do any of the children have pets? What do they think would be the one most important thing for their pet and what would be reflected in their pet's eyes? Now ask the children to think about themselves. If they were to draw their own eyes, what would be reflected in them? Take some suggestions from the class and use these to spark further ideas, and encourage children to reflect on themselves as individuals. Emphasise that everyone is different and that it sometimes takes a while before you can decide what is the *one* most important thing to yourself.

Give the children the oval-shaped black paper, the white eye-shapes and the chalk. Ask them to stick on the eyes and, when the glue is dry, to draw the one thing that is most important to them as a reflection in the eyes. Tell them to be thinking of this while they are pasting. Finally, tell them to use the chalk to add other details to the face – a nose, mouth, eyebrows and hair.

**Maggie Glen**

## *RUBY*

*Ruby* by Maggie Glen is a well-told story of a brave and optimistic toy bear who believes that being different means being special. The strong central character of the toy is appealing to young children. The illustrations and the variety in the way the text is laid out adds to the pace and excitement of the story. The dreadful prospect facing the toys, the daring escape and the happy ending make this an exciting and satisfying story for young children.

Read the whole story to the children, showing the illustrations to them and emphasising the changes in pace and atmosphere conveyed by the text divisions. This is the kind of story children will ask for again and again. Use the story tape to provide frequent opportunities for individuals or small groups to listen to the story. When children are familiar with the story, introduce the writing activities.

### About the author

Maggie Glen was born in Portsmouth. After graduating from the Loughborough College of Art and Design with an honours degree in fine art, she trained as a teacher and worked in both primary and secondary schools. She has written several very successful picture books including *Ruby* in 1990, *Ruby to the Rescue* in 1992 and *Ruby and the Parcel Bear* in 1995.

### Teaching content

All the bears are identical. There is no indication of character or appearance to make one bear stand out from the rest, except for Ruby. Ruby is interesting because she is different. Making characters different in appearance makes them more interesting to the reader.

### What you need

*Ruby*, chalkboard, writing materials.

### What to do

Show the children the picture of all the bears at the start of the book. Indicate a bear and ask one of the children to describe what it looks like. Then choose another bear and ask a child to describe that one. These descriptions will be repetitious because the only detail which is different is the colour of the bow around the bears' necks. In pairs, ask the children to look carefully at Ruby, describe her and say how she is different from the other bears. Give the children a few minutes to think about this and to rehearse the points they want to make. Then tell each pair to describe Ruby to the others. Ask the children if they think the descriptions of Ruby are more interesting than those of other bears. Can they explain what makes Ruby an interesting bear?

Next, write the starter sentence 'Ruby is an interesting bear because...' on the board and ask each child to write why they think Ruby is an interesting bear.

Paste the completed writing on to a large sheet of sugar paper and displayed in the story corner with a label, 'These writers think Ruby is an interesting bear. Do you agree?'

### Teaching content

Personal qualities are as important as appearance for characters. The author tells the reader about Ruby's qualities by describing what she thinks, what she says and what she does.

### What you need

Photocopiable page 206, A3 sugar paper, writing and drawing materials.

### What to do

Tell the children that all through the story the author tells us what kind of bear Ruby is by the way she describes what Ruby thinks, says and does. Take some suggestions from the children about what kind of bear they think Ruby is. Explain that the author has told us a lot about

Ruby's qualities and that we are going to find out how.

Give each child a copy of photocopiable page 206. Check that the children understand what each of the qualities at the bottom of the page means by asking them to explain them or to give an example of someone they know who has demonstrated these qualities. Then read through each statement given in the boxes on the photocopiable sheet. Explain to the children that you would like them to choose which qualities apply to the statements in the boxes. For example, they may think that the last statement tells us that Ruby was clever. They should therefore write the world 'clever' in the space at the right-hand side of the box. Some qualities may have more than one appropriate statement.

Ask the children to decide which quality they admired most about Ruby and then draw a picture of her demonstrating this characteristic. Underneath they should write what they liked best about Ruby. Pairs can take turns to draw or write. Let the children paste their completed drawings and accompanying statements side by side on an A3 piece of sugar paper.

## MY SPECIAL TOY

### Teaching content

Describing my toy (appearance, history, and characteristics) so that everyone knows what makes it special to me.

### What you need

A favourite soft toy which each child has brought to school, chalkboard, different-shaped blank labels (stars, circles, rectangles), wool, writing materials.

### What to do

The day before the activity, ask the children to bring a favourite soft toy to school. When they are choosing a toy to bring they should think about why it is a special toy. How would they explain to someone who had not met their toy why it is special to them?

Gather all the children and their toys together. Remind the children that Ruby was a special toy, but that all their toys are special in their own way. Explain to the children that each of the following points may make a toy special:

- it's name;
- the person who gave it to you;
- when you got it;
- where you got it;
- how it looks;
- how it feels when you cuddle it;
- how it acts.

Write these points on the board so that the children can refer to them.

Discuss each of these points with the whole group. Then put the children into pairs. Before they begin to talk to their partner, explain that they should think about each of the points above and decide how they will introduce and describe their toy. The children should then take it in turns to talk about their toy to their partner in the way which they have prepared. When all the descriptions are complete, show the children the labels and let them choose a shape they like for their toy. Tell them to write a label for their toy which states its name and gives one reason why it is special. Discuss some suggestions with the children, for example:

- It's special for cuddling.
- It has a cheeky face.
- It's my best friend.

Give the children time to write the label and attach it around the neck of their toy with wool. All of the toys could be placed along a shelf or on the top of a cupboard, each one showing its appropriate label.

## ESCAPE

### Teaching content

Telling the escape story from different points of view.

### What you need

A2 paper folded to form zigzag book, blank labels (made in different shapes), writing and drawing materials.

### What to do

Make the zigzag books that the children will use for the activity by using a sheet of A2 paper for each one, holding the paper sideways (landscape) and folding it in half vertically, then folding it in half again. When you open the paper out, there will be four inside pages. The reverse of page one of the zigzag book will be used for the title page. For each of the four pages draw a line horizontally across the page to indicate where children should draw (the top section) and where they should write (the lower section).

Reread to the children the part of the story where the bears escape, up to when they split up to go to different places to find new homes, or listen to this together on the story tape. Ask the children to work in pairs and to choose one of the bears. Give them a little time to make up their minds. They might choose a long-eared bear, a brown- and blue-eyed bear, a bear with a crooked smile, or a bear with an upside-down nose. When they have selected their bear, ask them to choose a name for it.

Tell the children that, in pairs, they are going to write the story of the escape from their bear's point of view, as if they were that bear and knew how it felt, what it said and what it did during the escape. Give each child a zigzag book and explain that their story will have five parts:
- out of the box;
- through the window;
- a new home;
- a good ending;
- the final stage – a title.

### Out of the box (page 1)
Write in the lower section of the first page:

I jumped out of the box with all the others. I said...

Tell the children to imagine that they were in the big box with all the bears when Ruby shouted, 'We'll escape.' Give the children time to think about their bear and how this bear might have felt at the start of the escape. Tell the children to draw a picture of their bear just as it was getting out of the box. While they are drawing they should think about how their bear felt and what it might have said. Underneath their drawing tell the children to complete the starter sentence you have given them, writing down what their bear said when it jumped out of the box. In their pairs the children should take it in turns to write and draw and to suggest ideas.

### Through the window (page 2)
Write in the lower section of the second page:

As I climbed through the window I thought...

Remind the children that getting through the window was the most difficult part of the escape. Discuss with the children why this was so. Give the pairs time to think about how their bear would react to this dangerous escape and to discuss it. Then tell them to draw a picture of the escape through the window, showing how their bear managed to get out. Then they should complete the sentence by describing what their bear thought as it was escaping.

### A new home (page 3)
Write in the lower section of the third page:

When I got to the...

Show the children the double-page spread where the bears arrive at a variety of safe places. Discuss each place with the children. Ask each pair to think about which place would be best for their bear. Then ask them to think about a new friend whom their bear might meet, or someone who might find the bear. Tell the children to draw a picture of their bear in a safe place and to write underneath it what their bear did when it arrived there.

### A good ending (page 4)
Write in the lower section of the fourth page:

Now I was...

Ask the children to think about what would make a good ending for their story. What would their bear do? How would their bear feel? What would it say at the end? Give the children time to think of some suggestions and discuss these with each pair. Now tell the children to draw a picture of the end of their story and to write the concluding sentence, beginning 'Now I was...'.

### The final stage – a title
Tell the children that now they have written their story they will have to think of a title for it. Remind the children that their story was about a special bear. Ask the children to remember what their bear was called.

Next, emphasise that the story was about an escape. Ask each pair to think about what would be a good title for their story. Give them time for discussion. (Remind the children that titles are usually short and may tell you something about the character of the story.) Then take some suggestions from the class. Give each pair a blank label like the ones used in the 'My special toy' activity. Now let the children make a final decision about the title for their story and then write this clearly on the label.

Tell the children to paste the title of their story on the front cover of their book and draw a picture of their bear. They should also write their own names to indicate that they are the authors.

Form groups of four from two pairs and let the children take it in turns to show their stories to their group and read them aloud.

## MR PAM PAM AND THE HULLABAZOO

*Mr Pam Pam and the Hullabazoo* by Trish Cooke is a story told by a young boy about a family friend, Mr Pam Pam. Mr Pam Pam is an exciting and humorous character.

> 'Mr Pam Pam is ever so tall, his arms and legs are stringy. He told me his favourite food is banana ice-cream with gravy.'

The story is about Mr Pam Pam's running joke – that he has seen a Hullabazoo – and is driven by the character of Mr Pam Pam and his relationship with the boy and his family.

As you read this book, young children will enjoy the repetition in it. Encourage them to join in with the repetition, and emphasise the rhythm as you read.

### About the author and illustrator
Trish Cooke was born in Bradford, West Yorkshire. She comes from a large family, all of whom provide her with the inspiration for her picture books: '... language is very important to me. I love music and rhythms and when people talk it is as if sometimes they are actually singing.' Trish Cooke is a well-known presenter on the BBC's television programme *Playdays*. She has also appeared on *You and Me* and hosted the radio programme *12345*. She has

acted in and written plays for television and theatre and has also written for *EastEnders*.

Born in Detroit, Michigan, Patrice Aggs came to Britain to study fine art. She now lives and works as an illustrator and printmaker in West Sussex.

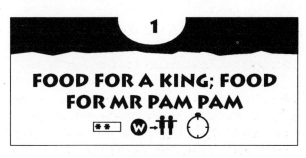

## FOOD FOR A KING; FOOD FOR MR PAM PAM

### Teaching content
Characterisation can be portrayed through what people say.

### What you need
*Mr Pam Pam and the Hullabazoo*, writing and drawing materials.

### What to do
Read to the children the whole story of Mr Pam Pam. Ask the children what they think of Mr Pam Pam. Do they like him? What sort of person do they think he is? Why? Where do they get this impression from? Do they know anyone who is a bit like Mr Pam Pam?

Now return to the first page of the story. Point out that at first we don't see Mr Pam Pam (he is in the distance), but we are told about him. Reread the first page to the children and ask what this indicates about Mr Pam Pam, establishing that it gives details of his physique ('ever so tall, his arms and legs are stringy'), what he does (looks after the baby) and what he says is his favourite food (banana ice-cream with gravy).

Do the children believe this really is Mr Pam Pam's favourite food? Why? Why do they think he says this? Ask the children to work in pairs and to suggest three other food combinations Mr Pam Pam might say he likes.

When most pairs have three possible food combinations, take some suggestions from the class. Then ask each pair to decide on the food combination out of their three that would best suit Mr Pam Pam, discussing it first. Give each pair a felt-tipped pen and ask them to write their choices on a piece of paper. Let the children illustrate their food combinations, which would enhance a wall display of the children's writing.

### Further development

The children could go on to collate their suggestions to make a menu or a cookery book for Mr Pam Pam.

## 2

## PAM PAM KNOCKING ON YOUR DOOR!

### Teaching content
Different characters say and speak differently and do different things.

### What you need
*Mr Pam Pam and the Hullabazoo*, photocopiable page 207, writing materials.

### What to do
After reading the children the story of Mr Pam Pam, return to page 3 of the story which describes what Mr Pam Pam does when no one answers the door. Are the words 'Pam Pam knocking on your door!' what they would expect him to shout through the letter-box?

Ask whether they know anyone who would shout through a letter-box. Point out that this is generally done by people who are quite outgoing characters and who know the household well. What would other people do if their knock on the door was not answered? What would the children do themselves?

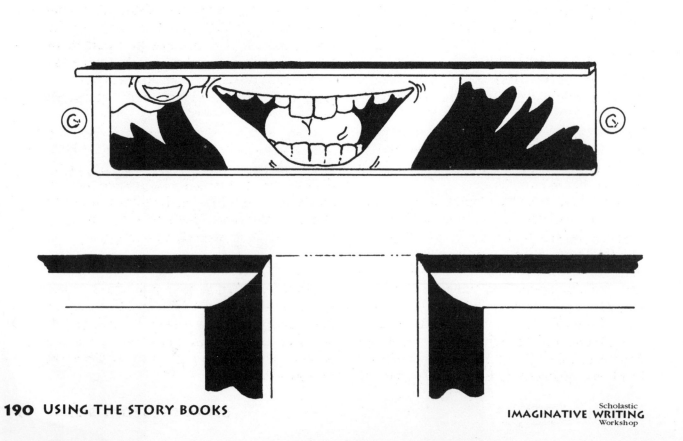

Give out copies of photocopiable page 207. Ask the children to work in pairs and to briefly describe which characters they think would shout through the letter-box and which would not. Are there some characters who would only shout through the letter-box in some circumstances? What would they say? Ask each pair to discuss the characters and then to share their answers with the rest of the class.

Next ask each pair to discuss what each of the characters pictured might say, either through the letter-box or to themselves as they turn away from the unanswered door. How would each character speak? Ask the children to write in the blank speech bubbles what they think each character would say.

Once they have finished, encourage the children to share their answers with the class. One child in each pair could then act out a person knocking at the door, and the rest of the class could try to guess who it is. The children could go on to discuss what each character would say to whoever opens the door. How would they say it?

## 3

## THE STORYTELLERS

### Teaching content
The stories people tell and find interesting reflect their personality and character.

### What you need
*Mr Pam Pam and the Hullabazoo*, photocopiable page 208, writing materials.

### What to do
Read the story of Mr Pam Pam to the children and remind them that it is about a long-running joke told by Mr Pam Pam.

Explain that from looking at Mr Pam Pam and listening to the sort of things he does and says, you imagine him to be the sort of person who would tell wild, funny stories about larger-than-life characters. Ask the children what other sorts of stories they think Mr Pam Pam would be good at telling or acting out. Why?

Give each child a copy of photocopiable page 208 and read through the story beginnings with the children. Explain that each person on the photocopiable sheet is a storyteller, but not

all the stories are there.

First of all, ask the children to match each story beginning to the person who they think is most likely to tell that sort of story. Ask them to do this individually and then to discuss the decisions they have made with a partner or friend. Why did they make those decisions? Ask each pair to come to an agreement about who is the teller of each story beginning that is given on the sheet.

Then, ask the children to consider the storytellers which have not been matched to a story beginning. What sort of stories do they think these people would tell? Why? The children could either suggest what the stories would be about, or they could identify a type of story which they think would be appropriate.

### Further development
• Ask the children to work individually, or in pairs, and to write a suitable story beginning for the characters they have been discussing.
• Do the children know of any adults who are good storytellers? Compile a class list. What sort of stories do they tell well?

## 4

## PAM PAM LOOKING FOR NEW CLOTHES!

### Teaching content
Choice of clothes indicates personality.

### What you need
*Mr Pam Pam and the Hullabazoo*, writing and drawing materials.

### What to do
Read the story of Mr Pam Pam to the children. Let them look closely at the illustrations and in particular at the clothes that Mr Pam Pam wears.

Tell the children to imagine that Mr Pam Pam needs some new clothes and that they will be going shopping with him. Ask each child to design a suitable shirt and a pair of trousers for Mr Pam Pam. What accessories do they think he would like to have? As the children draw or paint, ask them why they have chosen particular styles and colours, and ascertain what they think Mr Pam Pam would say about each item of clothing.

Cut out the clothes that the children have drawn or painted and make these into a display. Out of all the clothes, which item do they think would be Mr Pam Pam's favourite? Why?

### Further development
Choose one character from photocopiable page 208 and ask the class to design a new wardrobe for this person. Ask them to say why they think each item is suitable and what the person would say about his or her new clothes.

## 5

## MOVING LIKE A HULLABAZOO

### Teaching content
Vocabulary to describe movement.

### What you need
*Mr Pam Pam and the Hullabazoo*, space for movement (the school hall or gym), writing and drawing materials.

### What to do
In the school hall or gym, read the children the story of Mr Pam Pam. In particular, refer back to the section towards the end of the book where the reader meets the Hullabazoo. It is stated that 'he bounced and he twizzled – a lot, A LOT!' Can the children describe the various bounces and twizzles in their own words? If they get stuck you could suggest bounding, leaping, jumping, twisting, turning, flipping, stretching, spinning, vaulting, bending, springing, hopping, boomeranging, flying, hurdling, wriggling, flitting, spinning, skipping...

Now ask the children to think about the Hullabazoo doing other things. Ask them to consider some of the following actions and act them out:
- going up stairs;
- walking along the street;
- waiting to cross the road at traffic lights;
- putting the shopping away.

As the children experiment with each action, select a few children to demonstrate their ideas to the whole class. Each time try to get the children to describe exactly how they are moving. In this way, they will be building up a vocabulary for talking about movement.

After returning to the classroom, ask each child to draw and write about one of the situations detailed above. Tell the children to draw the Hullabazoo performing the action and then write a few lines to describe what he does and how he moves.

### Further development
What else do the children think that the Hullabazoo would do differently from other people? Make a list of the children's ideas and ask them to select one action, try it out, describe it and demonstrate it to a partner or the class, then draw it and write about it. This is a good activity for the children to do in pairs, if they choose.

# WHO'S BEHIND THE DOOR?

I'm going to put you to sleep for a hundred years

I'm going to turn your bed into nettles and thorns

I'm going to make you walk the plank

I'm going to stare at you with my black-eye patch

I'm going to make you green like me

I'm going to take you in my flying saucer

I'm going to make you wear rags

I'm going to steal your shoes

# IF YOU COME IN HERE

# IF YOU COME IN HERE

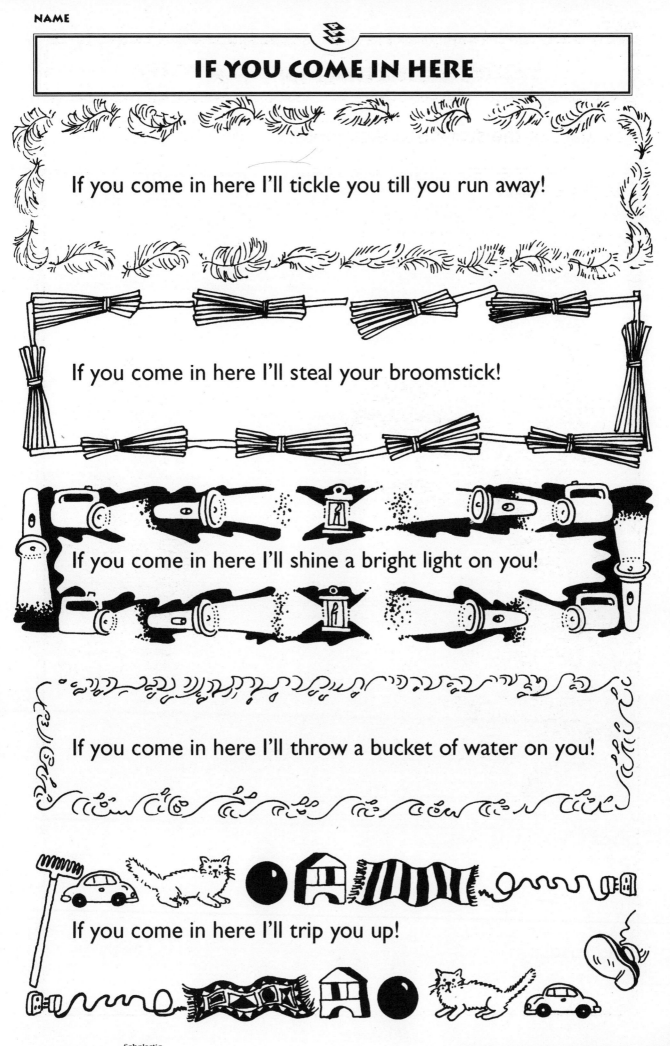

If you come in here I'll tickle you till you run away!

If you come in here I'll steal your broomstick!

If you come in here I'll shine a bright light on you!

If you come in here I'll throw a bucket of water on you!

If you come in here I'll trip you up!

# WORDS, PICTURES AND LAYOUT

The part of the story that was most

exciting was...



because...

happy was...



because...

sad was...



because...

heart warming was...



because...

# FIRST AND LAST

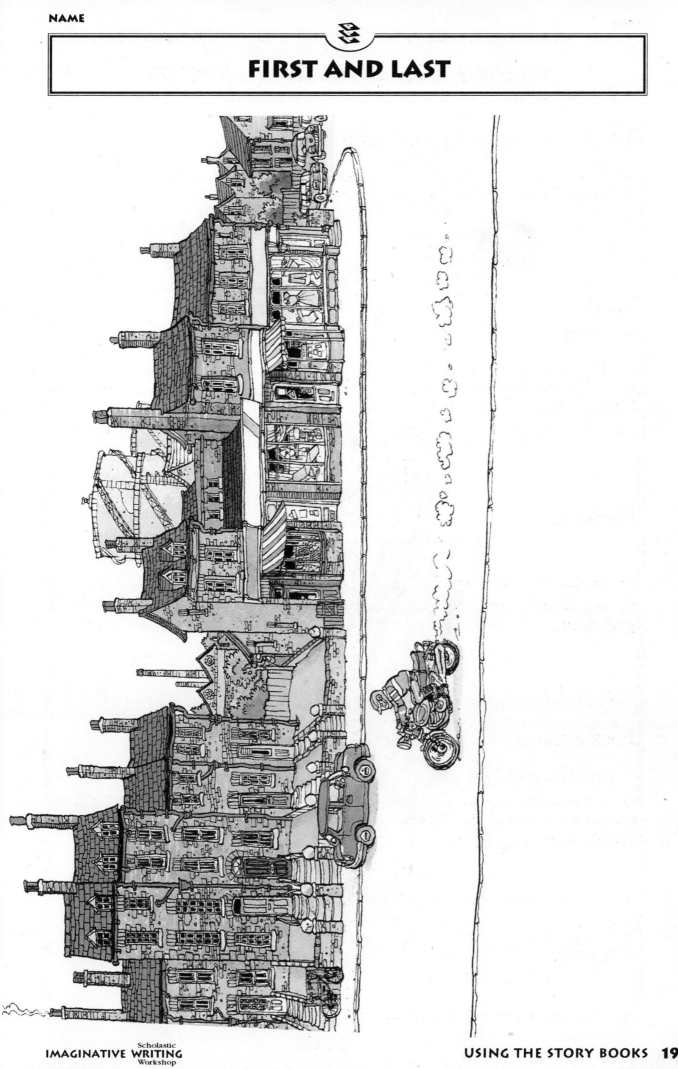

# CAT TALK

# EYES EVERYWHERE!

happy

not sure

looking around

angry

frightened

# IF I *MET* THE SCARY GHOST...

I would say

and then...

Scholastic
IMAGINATIVE WRITING
Workshop

# IN THE TORCHLIGHT

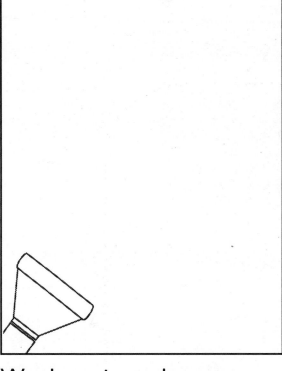

We shone it on the gate.

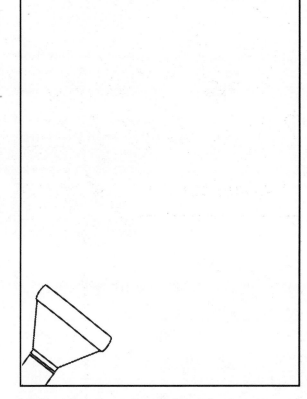

We shone it at the door.

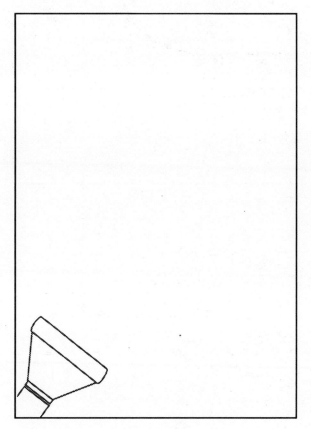

We shone it up the stairs.

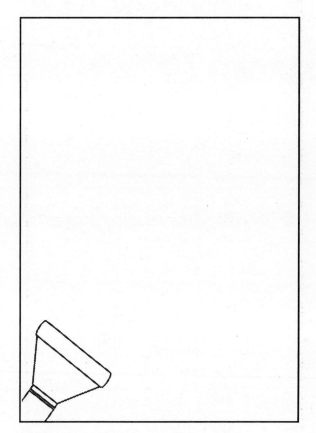

We shone it on the sign.

# SAFE AT LAST?

◆ Draw your own ending to the story about Tina and Tom.

◆ Write your ending here.

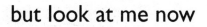

# WHEN I WAS LITTLE

◆ I looked like                    but look at me now

◆ I used to play with            but now I play with

◆ I used to say                      but now I say

# I DON'T LIKE IT WHEN OTHERS TELL ME...

Who says it?

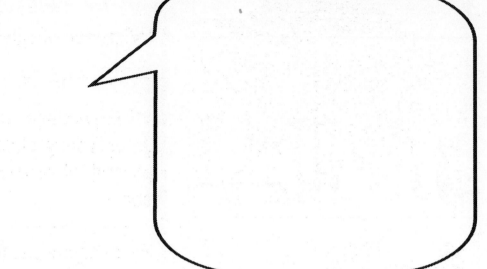

They say it because...

When they say it I...

# THE WAY HOME

Wizz out of school.

Walk through the school gates. Young children are playing while their parents chat.

Past the shops, full of busy shoppers and nice things to eat.

Past the shops, no time for sweets.

Through the park.

The park is full of children playing and shouting. Sunshine reflects on the boating pond.

Home at last. Time for juice and sandwiches

Garden gate. Home!

# WHAT KIND OF BEAR IS RUBY?

'That's *it*,' said Ruby again. 'We'll escape.'

Ruby wasn't surprised when she
was chosen from the other bears.

'YIPEE-E-E-E! "S" IS FOR SPECIAL,'
yelled Ruby.

Ruby climbed into the window of
the very best toy shop in town.

Ruby's fur stood on end;
she was horrified.

Hours passed. Suddenly Ruby
shouted, 'That's it!'

'There *is* no way out,' cried a
little bear. 'We're trapped.'
'This way,' shouted Ruby,
rushing into the cloakroom.

clever      brave      believes in herself   sometimes frightened

# PAM PAM KNOCKING ON YOUR DOOR!

# THE STORYTELLERS

## Story beginnings

Once upon a time when I was a child about your age...

Did you ever hear about the time when I was president of the United States of America? Well it happened like this...

A long long time ago there was a dark and deserted house. No one went there because it was supposed to be haunted...

Please Miss, Tom isn't going to go straight home from school like he's supposed to. He told me that he was going...